Celebrate!

NIGERIAN ART FOR THE COMMONWEALTH

The Official Exhibition for
The Commonwealth Heads of Government Meeting
Abuja, Nigeria, 2003

Organised by Sheeran Lock

This publication has been produced to
accompany the exhibition
Celebrate! Nigerian Art for The Commonwealth
shown at
The International Conference Centre, Abuja, Nigeria
5 - 8 December 2003
and open to the public
9 - 21 December 2003

Compiled and published in 2003 by Sheeran Lock
(www.sheeranlock.com)
ISBN 1 900123 90 8

SHEERAN LOCK

Catalogue edited by Imogen Lock
Editorial assistant: Sarah Wyke
Photography by Douglas Atfield, Abayomi Adeshida, Roderick Roy
Designed by Ray Fishwick
Printed by Suffolk Offset, UK

Exhibition curated by John Sheeran
Organised by Sheeran Lock, UK
Curatorial assistants: Alison Newell, Joanna Littlejohn, Fiona Mortimer

Advisory Group:
Ugo Uyah, Coordinator II, Commonwealth Heads of Government
    Meeting 2003 Task Force
John Sheeran, Sheeran Lock
Roderick Roy, Qua Tendis
Dr Chike Dike, Director-General of The National Gallery of Art, Nigeria
Dr Ayo Ighodaro, Bishopstone Associates

Cover illustration:
Chinwe Chukwuogo-Roy
Flame of the Forest 1999 (detail, Cat.6)

Celebrate! exhibition catalogue
sponsored by

MTN Nigeria

Celebrate! exhibition supported by

Biotec Laboratories Ltd.

Celebrate! education art materials
donated by

CONTENTS

FOREWORD

His Excellency Chief Olusegun Obasanjo
President, The Federal Republic of Nigeria

Today in the early years of the new millennium there is an increasing tendency to refer to the world as a global village; and we will continue to be shaped by the profound effects of globalisation as modern technology relentlessly drives us forward to a position in which the State is increasingly irrelevant. It has been assumed that all countries and all peoples will prosper through the breakdown of national frontiers, but while the industrialised countries remain the major beneficiaries, hardly any in Africa have been able to take advantage of the opportunities presented by this phenomenon. So it is even more imperative at this time to celebrate what makes us special and unique as Nigerians, not just as Africans or members of the modern Commonwealth, both of which mantels we wear proudly.

Nigeria as a nation is the sum of many parts, each unique in itself and each contributing to the wonderful richness of our shared culture. The *Celebrate!* exhibition features artists from the principal regions of our country, all of whose work is shaped by the traditions and history of their homelands. Its companion education programme benefits schoolchildren from all 36 states and from the capital Abuja, enabling them to exchange views with each other and with the wider world through the most powerful medium of all – art. The *Celebrate!* project is one of the most significant cultural events ever to have been organised in Nigeria, one which I hope will have a real and lasting effect on the way that we view and value our unique cultural identity.

Earlier this year I had the fortune to have my portrait painted by Chinwe Chukwuogo-Roy, one of Nigeria's, Africa's, and indeed the Commonwealth's most celebrated artists. It is a fascinating experience to see yourself as others see you, and the picture is included in this exhibition. Chinwe's joy in artistic creativity is apparent in everything she does – from her own paintings and prints; to support for other Nigerian artists; and to her vision for a sustainable art education programme for all our children. Her ambition is one I share and endorse wholeheartedly – to enable our young people to express themselves as individuals through their own creativity, so that art can once again take a central and vital role at the very heart of society in Nigeria. This is how we will maintain our own unique cultural identity in the face of the homogenising effects of the global village; and this surely gives us much to celebrate.

I am enormously grateful to Chinwe for all her efforts towards realising *Celebrate!*; to the Commonwealth Secretariat, and in particular the Secretary-General for his enthusiastic support; to Sheeran Lock for creating and managing the project so professionally; to MTN Nigeria and Biotec for their farsighted sponsorship; to Qua Tendis for its stalwart administrative assistance; to all my Ministerial staff and the CHOGM Task Force; and finally, to all the artists who generously lent pictures and sculptures to the exhibition and whose work should make us all proud to celebrate what it is to be Nigerian and to be part of the Commonwealth family.

Detail of Chinwe Chukwuogo-Roy's portrait of His Excellency Chief Olusegun Obasanjo, President, The Federal Republic of Nigeria

FOREWORD

The Right Honourable Don McKinnon
Secretary-General of The Commonwealth

It gives me enormous pleasure to contribute a foreword to this catalogue, which commemorates *Celebrate! Nigerian Art for The Commonwealth*, the official art exhibition for CHOGM 2003 in Abuja, Nigeria. Preparations for this unique cultural event can be traced back to March 2002 when I had the pleasure of unveiling the Commonwealth Golden Jubilee Portrait of Her Majesty Queen Elizabeth II painted by the distinguished Nigerian artist Chinwe Chukwuogo-Roy. It is included in this exhibition – the first time it has been seen outside the UK.

At the unveiling, Chinwe and I talked about the power of paintings to tell stories which cross cultural and language barriers, and about the positive role that art can play in encapsulating the culture of a country – its peoples and places, shared history and experience. Chinwe had already demonstrated her considerable skills in her Golden Jubilee portrait in which the spirit of the Commonwealth is expressed through references to the rich diversity of its member states.

I met Chinwe again in Manchester, UK, when I opened an exhibition of her paintings during the Commonwealth Games in summer 2002. By this time she had come up with an ambitious plan to celebrate her own country's cultural contribution to the modern Commonwealth through the eyes of its artists – from all regions of Nigeria. I am pleased that the idea was eagerly taken up by the CHOGM Abuja Task Force and the Nigerian Ministries of Culture and Education.

This catalogue gives a fascinating insight into contemporary Nigeria through its art and its shared artistic heritage. The education programme for schoolchildren which accompanies the exhibition, and which will continue long afterwards, expresses clearly the shared ambition of Nigeria and the Commonwealth to help its citizens, and especially young people, to lead more fulfilling lives and to express their thoughts about the world through the powerful and democratising medium of art in all its many forms.

Celebrate! has involved the efforts of many people and organisations, not least the fine artists whose work is featured; Ambassador Esan and his team at the CHOGM Abuja Task Force, notably Mrs Ugo Uyah, who has worked tirelessly; Sheeran Lock, which has organised the exhibition and produced this outstanding commemorative publication; Dr Chike Dike of the Nigerian National Gallery of Art; MTN Nigeria and Biotec for their generous sponsorship; Qua Tendis, without whose administrative support the project could not have been realised; and last, but not least, Chinwe herself for having the vision and determination to make it all happen.

The Rt. Hon. Don McKinnon with Chinwe Chukwuogo-Roy at the unveiling of the Golden Jubilee portrait of HM Queen Elizabeth II at Marlborough House, London, 2002 (Photo: Stephan Kneba)

CULTURE AND CREATIVITY

Chief Franklin Ogbuewu

Minister for Culture and Tourism, The Federal Republic of Nigeria

Culture and creativity help define us as a country and have done for successive centuries, from the earliest times. Art in all its many forms tells us about who we are and where we have come from, and can even help us glimpse where we might be going, however uncomfortable this can sometimes be. Artists are uniquely able to communicate across barriers – linguistic, societal, religious, and temporal – so that their work finds new meaning and resonance in each and every viewer. The *Celebrate!* project recognises the role art plays in uniting a diverse population, including as it does paintings, prints, drawings, and sculptures from many regions in Nigeria. The accompanying art education programme – for schools in all 36 states and the capital Abuja – underlines the important role of art and artists in Nigeria today and gives our young people a voice to express their hopes and fears for our country and the world in which we live.

The *Celebrate!* art education programme is being funded through sponsorship from the leading art materials manufacturer Winsor & Newton, which has kindly agreed to donate art materials to all the participating pupils and their schools. In addition, the exhibiting artists have generously agreed to contribute a percentage from the sale of their artworks towards the establishment of a long-term art programme for schools nationwide. We have looked at examples of Government best practice in the arts, and at Corporate Social Responsibility initiatives here and elsewhere which seek to engage with broad communities to the mutual benefit of all involved. The result is a simple yet sustainable programme which will encourage young people to take art seriously, and to consider it as a profession which has the power to transform lives and make a lasting difference.

The *Celebrate!* exhibition will be seen by visitors from all Commonwealth countries and this excellent publication will be distributed worldwide. We hope and trust that they present a visual argument for what makes our country special whilst communicating the shared values and aspirations of our Commonwealth family. This exhibition and publication give only a taste of the abundant artistic output of Nigeria today, and are intended to encourage people to delve deeper into our rich and varied culture – past and present – and support our young artists of the future.

One of the *Celebrate!* exhibition artists, Bisi Fakeye, at work

CELEBRATE NIGERIA

His Excellency Chief Emeka Anyaoku

I wanted to include a small tribute in this exemplary catalogue, because in essence the objective of the *Celebrate!* exhibition and education programme is the embodiment of something which I have long felt needed to be expressed to a wide audience: that Nigeria has many achievements to its name, not least its abundant creativity, and so has much to celebrate.

For many years during and post-colonisation, Nigerians have had to work in inauspicious circumstances to secure their futures and also to have their voices heard. Now we have embarked on the road to democracy we have much more to celebrate. All too often we read and watch news that accentuates the negative about Nigeria and about Africa in general. *Celebrate!* gives us the opportunity to spread positive news about what we hold dear. Nigerian artists today are continuing to create important statements which express their feelings for their country through myriad artistic styles and media, some drawing on tradition, others creating new forms, just as they have for centuries. It is only right that we should celebrate their achievements during CHOGM Abuja – a perfect international platform, attended by leaders representing a third of the world's population.

Some of the artists featured in *Celebrate!* are well known in Nigeria and beyond. Others are still establishing their reputations. I would particularly like to commend the work of two artists who have done much to champion the practice of art in Nigeria and to promote this work to a broader audience. Bruce Onobrakpeya is one of our best-known and most respected artists, and his work is included in many of the great international art collections. His support for up-and-coming artists – through practical workshops and forums, and now also through the development of an international art centre – is a selfless example that all should be encouraged to follow. It is a delight to see a broad selection of his work represented here.

On a more personal level, I have known Chinwe Chukwuogo-Roy for several years now and was privileged to have my portrait painted by her whilst I was Secretary-General of the Commonwealth. I am pleased to say that this commission led to Chinwe's work receiving wider recognition and ultimately played a part in her being commissioned to paint the Commonwealth Golden Jubilee portrait of the Head of the Commonwealth, Her Majesty Queen Elizabeth II, in 2002. Chinwe has been instrumental in bringing *Celebrate!* to CHOGM Abuja and in launching a sustainable art education programme which I hope will be implemented in schools throughout Nigeria.

Of course, all the *Celebrate!* artists make valuable contributions to the culture of our vibrant and diverse nation, and all are doing important work in maintaining Nigeria's artistic continuity. It is fascinating to see such a wide range of pieces by this talented group of artists, and all the more encouraging to realise that they represent a tiny proportion of our creative arts fraternity. I hope that the *Celebrate!* project will go some way to help reshape the image of Nigeria – and indeed Africa – in the minds of those from elsewhere who may be quick to judge and dismiss what they do not know or understand.

Chief Emeka Anyaoku with Chinwe Chukwuogo-Roy at the unveiling of his portrait, Marlborough House, London, 2000 (Photo: Joseph Kneba)

THE FINE ART OF COMMUNICATION

Adrian Wood
Chief Executive, MTN Nigeria

MTN is delighted to sponsor this superb commemorative publication, which accompanies the *Celebrate!* exhibition and art education programme launched at the Commonwealth Heads of Government Meeting 2003. Communications is our business. Our aim, which we are fast achieving, is to become the leading telecommunications operator on the African continent. But, of course, art is the most powerful communicator of all, as the artworks included in the exhibition, and reproduced in these pages, so admirably demonstrate.

This publication celebrates the cultural strength of the Federal Republic of Nigeria today. It gives a wonderful introduction to the richness of current contemporary art in Nigeria and sets this within the context of the millennia-old history of Nigerian artistic creativity and innovation. Both deserve to be much more widely known and we very much hope that the *Celebrate!* initiative will be the first of many, and that this catalogue will be read and treasured throughout the Commonwealth and beyond.

The MTN Group Foundation, launched in December 2002, has four principal areas of focus: arts, culture and heritage; education; science and technology; and HIV/AIDS. Our sponsorship of *Celebrate!* is an extension of our arts and education programme, which in South Africa currently includes the first private collection of African art to be taken into schools for educational purposes; the innovative New Contemporaries awards for up-and-coming artists; the Young Curators programme for secondary and tertiary learners; the first Artist-in-Residence programme in the private sector; and the first corporate link with the Department of Education in rewriting the arts curriculum. We hope very much to introduce similar initiatives in Nigeria based on this model. *Celebrate!* gives us a forum for communicating with leading artists, curators, educators and decision-makers who can help make this dream become a reality.

Corporate citizenship is a key to ensuring economic and social sustainability in the societies in which we operate, and we are proud of the investment we make to the Nigerian economy – in excess of $1.4 billion – and in community projects across Nigeria and the whole African continent. At MTN, the challenge is to link up every city, village, hamlet, river and creek in Nigeria. We subsist on the core values of integrity, friendliness, innovation, simplicity and a 'can do' attitude. We pride ourselves on the ability to make the impossible possible – connecting people with friends, family and opportunities. *Celebrate!* connects the work of seven outstanding artists with a national and international audience – with school children all over Nigeria, with 54 Heads of Government, with the Nigerian public and, through the mass media, with an untold number of people worldwide. We are proud to have played a part in making this happen and to be associated with such a worthwhile and imaginative venture.

BIOTEC

MAKING A DIFFERENCE

Ian Dalgleish
Chairman, Biotec Laboratories

Biotec is delighted to sponsor this important exhibition which presents highlights of contemporary Nigerian art to a world audience. We are especially pleased to be founder-benefactors of the *Celebrate!* art education programme for young people throughout Nigeria, which so closely complements our own company mission statement: 'we are here to make a difference.' We believe the initiative will make a real difference in stimulating creativity, unlocking talent, and raising personal aspirations and expectations in those who take part. The creative industries can be hugely beneficial for the economy of a country, and Nigeria is justly proud of its rich artistic and cultural heritage. *Celebrate!* links young people to the best artistic traditions of the past, introduces them to the work of some of the foremost artists of today, and creates new opportunities for them to 'make a difference' in years to come. Each will have his or her own distinct vision and means of expression, and we very much look forward to seeing the art which comes out of the education programme and listening to what the young people have to say.

Fundamental to Biotec is our commitment to the Commonwealth. This has grown during the last 20 years to a position where we are now actively encouraging investment from within the countries we serve, so that the company may eventually be owned by those who benefit most from our products, research and development. We have a presence in all 54 Commonwealth member countries where we develop, manufacture, and market medical diagnostics kits for testing in hospitals, laboratories, and at the bedside. Our research and development, carried out in several African and Asian countries as well as in the UK, has enabled us to produce revolutionary and dramatically improved TB testing systems that can bring about the saving of hundreds of thousands of lives by facilitating rapid treatment of the world's worst killer disease. We are currently developing kits for testing those hardest to analyse yet most vulnerable to the disease: the old and the young. Children are our future. Biotec is proud to help 'make a difference' by providing them with additional opportunities – surely a cause to *Celebrate!*

THE COMMONWEALTH

The International Conference Centre, Abuja, venue for CHOGM 2003 and the *Celebrate!* exhibition.

The Commonwealth is a unique global family comprising a voluntary association of governments and people of 54 independent countries around the world. From Africa to Asia, from the Pacific to the Caribbean, from Europe to North America, the Commonwealth's 1.7 billion people make up nearly 30 per cent of the world's population. Over half of the Commonwealth's peoples are aged 25 or under. The modern Commonwealth evolved out of Britain's imperial past and, today, it helps to advance democracy, human rights, and sustainable economic and social development. With English as a common working language and similar systems of law, public administration and education, the Commonwealth has become a vibrant and growing association of states in tune with the modern world.

Commonwealth countries work together to improve the lives of their citizens. In the words of the Commonwealth Secretary-General, Don McKinnon: 'One of the strengths of the Commonwealth lies in the values shared by its members. These values are enshrined in the 1991 Harare Principles. Whatever our individual religious beliefs, our cultural backgrounds, our national history, we all share the same commitment to foster human rights and tolerance, to promote democratic practices and to eradicate poverty.'

Commonwealth Heads of Government meet every two years to discuss how best to achieve their common goals. Meetings at ministerial and official level also take place throughout the year in different member states. Commonwealth professional associations and non-governmental organisations also play a central role in improving the lives of Commonwealth people. They do so in areas such as education, housing and health.

Celebrating diversity is one of the Commonwealth's basic tenets. The rich diversity in areas such as culture, history, race, religion, and ethnicity, reflects the varied membership of its 54 members. Stuart Mole, Director-General of the Royal Commonwealth Society, comments: 'The Commonwealth sees its diversity not as a weakness but as a source of strength and a cause for celebration. On numerous occasions the Commonwealth has consciously used its diversity to help bridge deep differences and defuse situations of real conflict.'

www.thecommonwealth.org

CHOGM ABUJA 2003

The 54 Commonwealth leaders meet every two years in a different Commonwealth country to discuss matters of common interest and progress initiatives to benefit the Commonwealth's diverse membership. This summit is called a Commonwealth Heads of Government Meeting or CHOGM. A CHOGM is arguably the only international forum where such a diverse group of countries with differing levels of capacity and resources come together as equals to find common positions through consensus, in a relatively informal manner. International programmes and other initiatives promoting democracy, racial equality, conflict resolution, cultural diversity, education, economic development, and access to modern technology are key areas of achievement from the 30-year history of CHOGMs. Not surprisingly, these summits provide fundamental direction for the modern Commonwealth. A communique of mandates and policies is issued at the end of each CHOGM. Declarations or statements on important matters are also issued by the leaders.

CHOGM is being hosted for the first time by the Federal Republic of Nigeria in 2003. It is taking place in its capital city Abuja at the International Conference Centre. The last CHOGM held in Africa, in Durban in 1999, marked a turning point in the history of the modern Commonwealth. Firstly, it marked 50 years of the association. Secondly, it heralded two landmark events: the completion of the South African democratic transition in 1994, which the Commonwealth had doggedly pursued for 35 years or so; and the return of Nigeria to a democratically elected government in 1999.

While the Commonwealth has carved for itself roles in science and technical cooperation, long-distance education, sports, and, lately, technical assistance in the area of debt management, it is at the political front that its achievements have been most influential. The Commonwealth's latest initiatives include the creation of the Commonwealth Ministerial Action Group (CMAG); election monitoring in member countries (by 2000, it had monitored more than 30); the engagement of 'civil society' in expanding democracy, and creating programmes especially to address the concerns of its smaller member states.

The Federal Government of Nigeria set up a National Task Force, headed by Ambassador Aderemi Esan, Minister of State for Works and Housing, to organise CHOGM 2003 in Abuja.

www.chogm2003.org

The entrance to the International Conference Centre, Abuja.

ABUJA CITY

Like Canberra and Brasilia, Abuja is a new purpose-built capital city and is located at the centre of Nigeria, Africa's most populous nation. Even though the city is growing quickly, it is less congested and polluted than the former capital, Lagos. It is an attractive city with flowering bougainvillea and exotic trees around its many office blocks, apartment buildings and villas. The focal point of Abuja is Aso Rock, a granite monolith which towers over the gleaming green dome of Nigeria's new National Assembly Building. Abuja is also a convenient jumping-off point for visiting other parts of Nigeria. Large diplomatic, business and cultural gatherings take place at the International Conference Centre, the venue for the Commonwealth Heads of Government Meeting 2003 and of the exhibition *Celebrate! Nigerian Art for The Commonwealth*.

www.abujacity.com

Above: view of Abuja with Aso Rock.
Left: the Abuja sports stadium and velodrome.
Opposite: view of Abuja.

THE CELEBRATE! EXHIBITION

John Sheeran

Celebrate! Exhibition Curator

The *Celebrate!* exhibition comprises over 100 works of art by seven contemporary Nigerian artists displayed at the International Conference Centre in Abuja for the Commonwealth Heads of Government Meeting (CHOGM) in December 2003. Seen by over 50 Presidents and Prime Ministers and their delegations, and afterwards by the public, it presents some of the best of contemporary Nigerian painting and sculpture.

The idea for the exhibition came in 2002 from one of the exhibiting artists, Chinwe Chukwuogo-Roy. When she discovered that CHOGM 2003 was to take place in Nigeria, Chinwe approached the UK-based art and communications consultancy Sheeran Lock to see whether it would be feasible to organise an exhibition of Nigerian art for CHOGM with accompanying publication, education programme and international publicity. Sheeran Lock has a long track record of organising such projects. It organised *Our World in the Year 2000: The United Nations Millennium Art Exhibition,* which was opened by UN Secretary-General Kofi Annan at the UN headquarters in New York. The exhibition featured pictures by over 250 artists from 50 countries and was praised by Mr Annan as: 'a splendid example of how the universal language of art can cross boundaries and barriers, bringing nations together to promote greater understanding among peoples and cultures.'

Chinwe knew Sheeran Lock's work well, for the company had helped to organise and promote the unveiling at Marlborough House, London, of her Commonwealth Golden Jubilee portrait of HM Queen Elizabeth II in March 2002. Later that year Sheeran Lock also organised *Chinwe: An Exhibition for The Commonwealth Games in Manchester*, opened by the Rt. Hon. Don McKinnon, Secretary-General of the Commonwealth, and widely acclaimed as one of the most impressive cultural events of the Games.

After meetings with representatives of the Nigerian High Commission and the Commonwealth Secretariat in London, and with the CHOGM Task Force and the Nigerian Ministries of Culture and Education in Abuja, the *Celebrate!* project was chosen as an official cultural event to mark CHOGM Abuja 2003. The plan was for *Celebrate!* to bring the peoples of Nigeria together through their art. It was decided to show the work of artists from different parts of the country, from the well-established to the up-and-coming. It was also important that the exhibition should feature different art forms, subjects and styles: from oil and acrylic painting, pastel and printmaking to sculpture in wood and bronze; from figurative to abstract work; and from realism to expressionism. The Director-General of the Nigerian National Gallery of Art, Dr Paul Chike Dike, was consulted about which artists to include and a selection was made which comprised Bruce Onobrakpeya, Bisi Fakeye, Nkechi Nwosu-Igbo, Samuel Uloko Onyilo, Mu'azu Mohammed Sani, and Fred Archibong. All were keen to participate in such a major showpiece of Nigerian art and some were able to complete new pieces in time for the exhibition.

As planning for the exhibition got underway, there were some exciting developments. The Commonwealth Secretariat agreed to lend Chinwe's portrait of Queen Elizabeth II, Head of The Commonwealth (Cat.17), which hangs at Marlborough House, meaning that for the first time the portrait would be seen outside the UK and in Africa. The Commonwealth also agreed to lend Chinwe's portrait of Chief Emeka Anyaoku, the Nigerian former Secretary-General of the Commonwealth (Cat.5).

He has been a keen supporter of Chinwe's art for some years and she admires him greatly for his achievements not only within the Commonwealth, but also within Nigeria and throughout Africa.

With only three months to go before the exhibition opened, Chinwe approached His Excellency Chief Olusegun Obasanjo, President of the Federal Republic of Nigeria, to ask whether he would agree to her painting a portrait of him. The President not only accepted but also lent his full support to the *Celebrate!* project. Chinwe planned to hang the portrait of the President alongside her portrait of the Queen. Her intention was for the two portraits – which personify Nigeria and the Commonwealth – to hang side-by-side as a symbolic representation of the CHOGM meeting. She therefore painted the portrait of the President exactly the same size as that of the Queen and framed it the same way so that they would be seen as companion pieces. The pictorial composition also mirrors the Golden Jubilee portrait, with the President shown full-length in his robes standing in a Nigerian landscape (Cat.50).

The final piece of the *Celebrate!* jigsaw-puzzle was to establish an education programme which would enable the exhibition to be used as a catalyst throughout Nigeria, Africa and the wider Commonwealth to show the importance of art and its practice as a means of self-expression among young people. Chinwe greatly admired a national art education programme called *Talking Pictures* which Sheeran Lock had organised in 2002-3 in tough inner-city schools throughout the UK to introduce pupils to their British and European heritage. Teenagers who had never been to an art gallery before or seen an original painting, let alone met an artist or painted in oils, were given the opportunity to do so. The results were outstanding, not only as a reflection of the pupils' artistic achievement and their increased awareness of the importance of their own culture,

but crucially for giving them new commitment, enthusiasm, sense of purpose, and self-worth.

Chinwe's own teaching in schools had made her well aware of the impact that quality art materials and tuition can have on young people's interest and performance – but few schools can afford them. For the *Celebrate!* exhibition in Abuja, she therefore planned to do something which was both symbolic and would open people's eyes to the potential of young people's creativity. Rather than go to schools in Abuja to teach, she decided to work with the Nigerian Ministry of Education and invite a representative selection of young people from all the 36 states of Nigeria and the capital Abuja to come to the exhibition, all expenses paid. After a conducted tour of the exhibition led by Chinwe, she planned to introduce them to the other *Celebrate!* artists, before taking them into the CHOGM Conference room, only recently vacated by the Heads of Government, but now transformed into a studio in which the young artists could draw and paint. Chinwe decided to work alongside the children on an unfinished painting entitled *Children of the Commonwealth* so they could observe and learn at first hand what and how she painted. The media would be invited so that images of the art masterclass could be broadcast to a national TV audience.

Celebrate! is one of many initiatives now being taken in Nigeria to promote visual art not just within the country itself but to an international audience. It is an important element in the drive by Nigeria to promote its historic and contemporary culture. Much from the past is, of course, held in museums in the West and some has been placed on UNESCO's Red List of cultural objects due for repatriation. Much from the present is less known and appreciated and the *Celebrate!* exhibition champions the quality of work being produced by Nigerian artists today.

NIGERIAN ART AND THE COMMONWEALTH

Chinwe Chukwuogo-Roy in discussion with John Sheeran

The following discussion between Chinwe Chukwuogo-Roy and the *Celebrate!* exhibition curator John Sheeran, took place in the artist's studio on 23 September 2003.

JS   *Can you start off by you explaining why you think art is important and what purpose you think it serves?*

CCR   From when I was a little girl in Awka, I can remember walking down the village road just running my finger along a wall because I liked the shape and the variation. It was something fantastic for a child to grow up surrounded by sights, sounds, colours, patterns, and textures. I grew up to understand that they were special to where I lived. And they would be different if I went to another town or village. I think it is sad that a lot of this has gone now. For hundreds of years, artists were at the centre of the community producing all sorts of work – painting a house, carving a door, making the village drums or creating a sculpture. But this tradition has almost died out. You no longer see art everywhere and artists are no longer recognised and valued as they were before. In fact, art is not really seen as a proper profession by many people in Nigeria today. It is looked down upon.

But art and artists are the essence of the culture of a people. When we are all dead and gone, what is it that remains from our time? Future generations will judge us as much from our culture as anything else. But also for each of us during our own lives, art is something to fall back on. Art is something that gives you joy. It gives you hope and makes you think about who you are and even why you are. It saddens me to see society abandoning its culture because of materialistic 'progress'. Nigeria cannot afford to miss out on its art. If people find out about our culture, then they discover about us and what we are

all about. It helps them to understand our concerns and maybe even identify with us. A flourishing and diverse culture is a sign of a civilised and balanced society.

JS   *The cultures of the various peoples which make up Nigeria go back thousands of years. The region was a meeting point of transcontinental migration routes so the country has an amazingly rich diversity of customs, traditions and language. You only have to look at the Benin bronzes or the ancient Nok sculptures, or the Ife bronze and ceramics and Igbo-Ukwu finds to realise just how sophisticated and wide-ranging the art of Nigeria is. You are passionate about Nigerian art, both past and present. What aspects particularly appeal to you ?*

CCR   You are right. Nigerian art can stand up to any other culture in the world. But it is not just Igbo art or Nigerian art in all its many strands that interests me. I am passionate about all cultures in Africa. I started teaching myself about African history and culture in the 1980s. At the same time I became more aware of current events in Africa – the wars, dictatorships, the destruction of communities and of ways of life that had existed for centuries. I have experienced man's inhumanity to man and the horrors of war from first hand. So art has gradually become a vehicle for me to express my own feelings about all of this. It has been a natural progression.

When my father died, I was deeply moved by the way his life was celebrated at his funeral with traditional Igbo dress, music and ceremony. I sensed that I might never see the like of it again and I was determined to do a series of pictures on the subject. I am so pleased that you have chosen two of them for the *Celebrate!* exhibition (Cat.2 & 3). It is just one of many aspects of our culture which are rapidly disappearing. But we

Chinwe sketching children in the Lokoja Fish Market beside the Niger River, Nigeria

Chinwe with Mrs Ugo Uyah (left), CHOGM Task Force, visiting the Akwete Weavers' Cooperative, Abia State, Nigeria

exhausted. But I also realised that a whole new avenue had opened up for me as far as my art was concerned. I knew what my purpose in life was and what my art should be about. That's when I began *Our Past, Our History* (Cat.4), part of my *Africa Past, Present and Future* series of paintings, which will be ongoing and probably take me the rest of my life!

JS *I can understand why you think that cultural identity is so important. If you don't know where you have come from, how can you know where you are, or where you are going? But why do you think it is important for all Nigerians, and all Africans, to be aware of their national, regional and local history and culture?*

CCR It's a sad fact that most current African countries' histories go back only a short distance to colonial times – in Nigeria's case when the region was colonised by the British. Nowadays, you could be forgiven for thinking that Nigeria is expected to do everything according to Western standards. Why should we abandon what we are, to be what others want us to be? You could argue that one of the reasons why we are failing is because we are leaving behind the essence of who we are.

JS *And, of course, Africa has lost a lot of evidence of those cultures too.*

CCR Absolutely. We have lost most of it. Just look in American and European museums. Much of our heritage is languishing in their storage rooms, hardly ever displayed. Africans wanting to discover their heritage and look at African antiquities have to get on a plane to London, Paris or New York. How many ordinary Africans can afford that? I have recently done a series of large monoprints on this subject called *Hidden Treasures* showing individual cities with African sculptures looming large over them and I am delighted that you have selected some of these for the *Celebrate!* exhibition (Cat.33-36).

And there is still, of course, the organised illegal trade in antiquities to cope with, involving unscrupulous dealers and supposedly respectable Western institutions. So the little we

have had our own way of doing things which has served us for millennia – why should it be relegated to something 'we once did in the past'? I had to record my father's funeral and I felt at the time I wanted to record other examples of African culture.

Then when Kris Akabussi commissioned me to do a series of paintings about the African slave trade and its impact on the lives of countless individuals, I started by reading over 60 books on the subject. It was such a horrendous period for all Africans. It was a profoundly disturbing experience to paint the pictures. After getting my thoughts and feelings down on the canvases, I felt a tremendous relief, though I was emotionally have left is slowly leaking away; and even what we have left, relatively few people are interested in. I must say, though, that at the moment Nigeria is working hard to get its antiquities back. But more work can be done. There should be more pressure applied. I imagine some museums around the world would be reluctant to lend their African treasures because they know just how important and central they are to the countries and cultures concerned.

JS *Do you see one of the purposes of your art as being to promote awareness of this situation?*

CCR   Well, if we have little remaining of our past culture, then it is even more important for our contemporary culture to be nurtured, kept alive, and supported with all it takes. It must not be tokenism. This is why the *Celebrate!* exhibition is so important. You can see examples of painting and sculpture by some of the best artists from different regions of Nigeria.

In my own work I make references to the past. I hope my work is a bridge for Nigerians and Africans to reconnect with their ancient cultures. I am trying to make the past relevant to today and to create something innovative from tradition. I just feel frustrated sometimes that most people who see my work and really take it in are those who are already converted and convinced by the message in the first place. Again, this is another reason why the *Celebrate!* exhibition is so important as there will be lots of people coming who will never have been to a museum or art gallery before – or probably ever seen original works of art. After the Heads of Government see it and the international conference is over, *Celebrate!* will be open to the people. Anyone can come and it's free. The word 'celebrate' sums up the attitude we must all have. Let's celebrate the work of our contemporary artists. Let's celebrate Nigeria. Let's celebrate the Commonwealth.

JS *Education is a way of getting the message across. You do a lot of educational work with young people. And for this exhibition there is a heavy emphasis on education and the participation of children. Can you explain what you are trying to achieve?*

Chinwe visiting a weaver's home in Akwete Village, Abia State, Nigeria

CCR   To me, education is the key to unlocking potential – and here I mean the potential of young people not only to understand the importance of their cultural identity and to appreciate great works of art, but to create their own art, to make their own statements, to contribute to their own culture. Children are our future. We have to make sure that our culture and our art are looked after for the generations to come. So let's start with the children. We need to make them understand

Chinwe teaching drawing at the Regina Pacis Girls Secondary School, Abuja Federal Capital Territory, Nigeria

is an essential ingredient for the future Nigeria. And I believe the same may be the case in countries and regions all over Africa, and indeed all over the world.

JS *When you were a child did you receive any encouragement in art ? How did you become an artist?*

CCR I've always said that I became an artist because I couldn't do anything else apart from draw. I've always drawn and painted – ever since I could pick up a pencil or brush. It gives me such joy. A turning point came when I was about eight years old. My father gathered all his children together to ask them each in turn what they wanted to be when they grew up. Everyone said what they hoped to be – a doctor, a lawyer , an accountant, an engineer, a teacher – the proper professions. I said I didn't want to be any of them. I wanted to be an actress or an air stewardess, but my father was having none of it. Then later I said to him: 'Well, I can draw, maybe I can be a drawer'. My father said ' Oh, you mean an artist?.' 'Yes', I said, 'I suppose so'. 'Oh', he said, 'That's fine. That's great – Leonardo da Vinci, Rembrandt, Van Gogh. You'll do well, my daughter!' I didn't know who these people were and only found out later at art college. I can now see my father had ambitions for me! My mother kept all my drawings – which gave me the feeling of their importance – until they were burnt in the Biafran war.

Young people are under pressure to conform to expectations and the goal of many parents is for their children to pursue careers in teaching, medicine or law, certainly not art. What is so sad is that there are children with talent whose creativity is never appreciated and allowed to flower. My mission is to make children aware of what they could be. If they have that talent, if they feel that creative instinct in them, then I want them to be encouraged to use it to the best of their abilities and to the benefit of their community.

JS *The education programme for the Celebrate! exhibition brings together children from the 37 different regions of Nigeria. They will be given a tour around the exhibition and then use the massive conference room used by the Heads of Government as a*

what this involves. At the moment in Nigeria there is little money for archaeological digs or establishing regional and national museums and galleries with the sort of staff and facilities you see in the West. This shows you how low a priority Nigerian cultural identity is given. This will never change unless children – the business and political leaders of the future – become convinced that cultural identity is important to their lives and *young artists' studio. This is a hugely symbolic statement about the role of art in bringing young people together for a common purpose.*

CCR   It's a small drop in the ocean, but it is something. It's a seed. I'm looking forward to teaching them. In the UK and Nigeria when I go into schools the teenagers often come up to me for a chat. They tell me that I'm a role model for them. That's great. They are thinking 'If she can do it, then so can I. That's what I want to be'.

JS   *And you can help them on their way. Some may end up as artists, or film animators, or in fashion, or in TV – and they will all be in creative professions, adding in their own ways to the cultural diversity of their country. It's also something very personal. How many people go through their lives wishing they had a fulfilling job in which they can be creative and express themselves?*

CCR   Absolutely. It is very important that we are all given the opportunity to develop the creative part of ourselves. In Nigeria, there are real problems with funding and facilities in education. They simply don't have the materials. I've been to schools with no art room – only pencils and paper, nothing else. It's a question of lack of money and priorities.

JS   *But couldn't Nigerian businesses be encouraged to buy art materials for the schools and to get involved with projects?*

CCR   Yes, they can help with funding. A business could give its name to funding art materials for a school. Wouldn't it be wonderful if this happened all over Africa? What a vision that would be for a multi-national company!

JS   *I would like to turn now to the Commonwealth. Some people might argue that the Commonwealth is irrelevant in this age – a collection of post-colonial, post-empire countries that have little in common other than that they were once ruled by a single power. You have made a particular point of championing the Commonwealth. The Commonwealth Heads of Government Meeting in Abuja presents you with certain opportunities for your own mission. Why is the Commonwealth such an important platform for you? What do you value in the Commonwealth?*

CCR   Well, I can understand why people might think that way about the Commonwealth. But I find such an attitude very upsetting. Why kick something that brings benefits to so many? I know what the Commonwealth does in numerous countries. It is not a colonial organisation. All the member countries have chosen to join. They all have a say in what happens. It's mutually beneficial. It's like a group of countries that have a similar history, trying to do things together in the modern world, so they can each make progress individually and collectively. What is wrong in that? When there are disagreements, problems, civil unrest, disasters, wars – which can, of course, happen in Commonwealth countries as in any other countries – they try to sort things out, like a family. Not everyone sees eye-to-eye, but there is still a common purpose. At least the Commonwealth provides an opportunity for discussion, understanding and hopefully compromise, if needs be.

The Commonwealth does a great deal of good in the world for which it gets little recognition. The Commonwealth Games in Manchester last year was an incredible event allowing smaller and poorer countries to shine on an international stage. We can learn about them through their sporting achievement, just as we can through their artistic achievement. This is why I thought it was so important to exhibit my paintings in Manchester during the Games. Anyone who attended the exhibition, which was filled with people from all over the Commonwealth, and heard the Secretary-General's opening speech, couldn't fail to see how relevant a body the Commonwealth is. It is definitely a case of what binds us together is stronger than what divides us.

To have the Commonwealth Heads of Government coming to Nigeria gives my country a chance to show itself off to the international community. So much of the news that comes out of Africa is bad news, but we have so many things to celebrate. Let's celebrate the Commonwealth. The other member countries are our brothers and sisters.

Chinwe sketching Broken Glass, a Fulani herdsman, on the road between Makurdi and Lokoja, Kogi State, Nigeria.

JS *The Commonwealth meeting is all about dialogue leading to understanding. Isn't this what the exhibition is all about too?*

CCR Yes. It's about dialogue with the other artists exhibiting; dialogue with the children; dialogue with the Heads of State; dialogue with the media; dialogue with everybody who comes to the exhibition. It's about being able to communicate and say: 'Yes. This is who we are and this is what we are doing'.

JS *Can you say something about the work you are exhibiting and what it reveals about you?*

CCR It's so difficult to comment on my own work. I just hope people enjoy my pictures and have their eyes, minds and hearts stimulated. I suppose my work shows that I'm a humanist. The exhibition includes a lot of portraits. I love people. I paint people. I work with people – whether it's my baby daughter or the Queen or President. I just enjoy the company of people. So that's an important message to get across. Then there's the message about Africa's history and culture. As I've mentioned, I'm interested in what we were, what we are, and what we are going to be. Then there are the Commonwealth pictures in which I am trying in a few images to put across my thoughts about the Commonwealth – about its being a collection of different peoples working together for a better future. I'm currently working on a picture on the theme of children of the Commonwealth.

JS *There are six other artists exhibiting. Why is that important to you?*

CCR Because it shows the world that Nigeria has some extremely gifted artists, some well-known, some less so. It sheds light on their work, and of course brings it to the attention of Nigerians too. The exhibition gives only a flavour of what Nigeria has to offer. But the hope is that people will spread the word, and be encouraged to return. The exhibition is also being seen by key decision-makers from within Nigeria, from other African countries and from other states around the world.

JS *Finally, I want to return to something you were talking about earlier in our discussion – the community as a binding agent in society. Would it be accurate to describe your art as a visual expression of community?*

CCR   To answer that question, I want to go back to the way people come to be where and what they are. To survive and establish a community, people have to live, work, and do things together. They work everything out based on their individual and collective experience. Over a long period this experience becomes tradition and culture. In a true community, each person needs the other, whether to sell to, to buy from, or whether just as a shoulder to cry on or as someone to give them love. You need other people to survive.

The community is just a wider family in a diverse society. I am Chinwe Chukwuogo-Roy, wife and mother; then I am Igbo; then I am Nigerian; then I am African; then I am a Nigerian living in England. So this sense of community is very important to help you become and understand what you are. As my art is also who I am, yes, you can say that my art is about community. There are many communities in my life, and I thank the community of the Commonwealth and the community of Nigeria for giving me the opportunity to exhibit with my fellow Nigerian artists at such a prestigious event. It means an enormous amount to me.

JS *Thank you, Chinwe.*

Chinwe presenting Councillor Roy Walters, Lord Mayor of Manchester, UK, with a copy of her biography at her exhibition during the Commonwealth Games, Manchester in 2002

NIGERIAN ART: PAST, PRESENT AND FUTURE

Dr Paul Chike Dike

Director-General of The National Gallery of Art, Nigeria

Introduction

Nigeria, with a population of more than 100 million people, and over 250 languages, is the most populous and diverse country in black Africa, a diversity that finds its fulfilment in common and shared cultural characteristics and a proud and timeless heritage of creative artistic achievement. Although archaeologists have dated Nok, Nigeria's oldest documented art tradition, at more than two thousand years – a period long enough to justify claims of a great civilization in the Nigerian plateau – there are several undated cultural and artistic finds that suggest a creative distinction that could date from the first origins of man on the planet. Two examples are the Akwanshi stone monoliths of the Cross River area of Nigeria and the Esie soapstone images. The latter came to world attention through collections made by the German ethnologist Leo Frobenius in 1911 and are believed to be timeless in age, despite traditions that claim that the images are representations of white-skinned strangers whose attempts to attack the local Chief, the Elesie, resulted instead in them being turned into stone by mystical forces. A more authentic tradition documented by the archaeologist and ethnographer, Ekpo Eyo, seems to suggest that when the people of Esie migrated from old Oyo during Abiodun's reign as Alafin or King (c.1775) they found these figures made of steatites or soapstone[1]. Similarly the Akwanshi carved monoliths represent a tradition that died out by 1900 and are said to represent the images of the ethnic or village ancestors of the Nta, Nselle and Nnam groups of the Cross River area who own them. In terms of historical dating and chronology, however, it is significant that the story of their origins and date have been lost with time, which in itself provides a clue as to the depth of their antiquity.

Head 1st-2nd century BC
Nok terracotta
The National Commission for
Museums and Monuments, Lagos

Head Pendant 10th century
possibly Igbo, bronze
The National Commission for
Museums and Monuments, Lagos

It is these great cultural and artistic achievements of the Nigerian people that constitute our shared cultural and artistic heritage which flourished long before European incursions. These include great monumental sculptures, paintings, ceramics, pottery, and earthenware, and the making of murals, textiles and clothing, rock paintings, and architectural designs and drawings, which were made in virtually every nook and cranny of the country. Art was an integral part of life in the pre-colonial period and where artists ranked higher than other professional groups.

Important Nigerian artistic achievements include the famous Tsoede bronzes of the Lower Niger; the figurines and sculptures of the Dakakari of Kebbi State, and of the Yelwa of Borno State. In addition, there is a whole range of traditional art of the Yoruba of the south-west made up of ancient staffs, stools, masks and masquerade attires, carved doors and house posts, presentation and offering bowls and pots, many of which were recovered at archaeological sites. The majority are in ethnographic collections. In the Nigerian southern east, the Igbo artistic achievements include paraphernalia of title-taking: chieftaincy stools, and staffs of office, particularly for men of the Ozo title society; drums for ritual and social music; and the famed Ijele masquerade that conceptualises the world around.

Other Nigerian groups also demonstrate distinguished creative cultural attainments. Ethnographers have documented the artistic and decorative Anjenu figures of the Idoma people of the Benue valley. The Ekoi people of the present Cross River State are distinguished for their skin-covered masks, a tradition shared with the neighbouring Camerounian peoples. In the present Rivers State of Nigeria are the Ogoni, a small ethnic group of about 500,000 people reputed for the distinction of their dance masks, whose neighbours, the Ijaw, are renowned for their Ejiri wooden figures that serve religious purposes.

Like their southern brothers, many of the ethnic groups of what is geographically known as northern Nigeria, also produce masks for ritual and ceremonial purposes, and sculptures mainly for religious purposes. The Mambila, Montol and Waja figures are truly representative of the cultural traditions of the central

Ceramic Vessel 10th century
Igbo, fired clay
The National Commission for
Museums and Monuments, Lagos

region of northern Nigeria, an area occupied by numerous small and diverse groups that share many of the cultural traditions and attitudes of both the farthest north and the south of Nigeria. The Mama of the Wamba local government area of the present Nasarawa State are known for their fertility dance called Mangam, for which they make masks representing images of bush cows with long horns. Similarly the Mumuye people of the present Taraba State are the proud owners of horned masks used for religious supplications of nature cults, while the Vadosun cult is symbolised by a carved calabash horn, and a further cult, the Vabo, is symbolised by horned masks[2].

Highlights of Nigerian Traditional Art

The apogee of Nigerian traditional artistic attainment is best represented by four major traditions that have earned world attention, namely: Nok, Igbo-Ukwu, Ife, and Benin. The interesting point about these four civilizations is that they synchronise with various periods of artistic attainment in the Nile Valley, Mesopotamia, and the great traditions of European artistic heritage. While Nok, for example, flourished during the period that coincided with the construction of the Parthenon (c.340 BC) and the Temple of Dendur (c.15 BC), Igbo-Ukwu bronze civilization reached its pre-eminence at the same period as the construction of the Great Mosque at Damascus 705 AD. Ife bronze art coincided with the construction of the famous Notre Dame Cathedral in Paris (c.1163-1200 AD), while Benin flourished during the construction of the Taj Mahal in India (c.1630-48 AD)[3]. While Nok is thought to be an iron-working civilization that flourished around 500 BC, the finds are essentially clay objects and beads, appropriately described as terracotta culture, while the other three represent bronze traditions. A brief explanation of each of these follows.

Nok

About 150 sculptures recovered in the small village of Nok in the present Plateau State of Nigeria are the earliest sculptures to have been found in the whole of sub-Saharan Africa. The finds came about as a result of a combination of chance ethnographic collections made by nine workers as well as intense archaeological exploration. They represent some of the finest material artefacts in traditional Nigerian art. It is generally believed that Nok might be even older than 2,000 years because some radiocarbon dating has produced even earlier dates[4]. This dating work is still inconclusive but supports the theory of a timeless artistic heritage of the Nigerian people. Nok is distinguished by several unique characteristics, including the use of geometric forms, namely cylinders, cones and spheres, to depict animals and human beings, as well as the piercing of the eyes, mouth, nostrils, and ears. The eyes are usually circular or triangular in shape, while the eyebrows balance the sweep of the lower lids. There is usually a carefully crafted depiction of jewellery and hairstyle.

Igbo-Ukwu

Igbo-Ukwu is the oldest bronze tradition in Nigerian art. The works recovered from various archaeological sites are stylistically peculiar and dissimilar to the other bronze traditions of Ife and Benin. Using the lost-wax method, Igbo-Ukwu artists produced a whole range of bronze objects including roped pots, ornaments, staffs, and insignia of office. The numerous works included ritual vessels, staff heads and ornaments found in a shrine and also, more importantly, in what is thought to be the burial chamber of the Eze Nri at Oraeri, a small neighbouring town to Igbo-Ukwu. Their experience of internecine warfare and population movement seems to suggest that the Igbo-Ukwu finds were really items of Nri culture.

Ife

The distinction that marks Ife artistic attainments is best illustrated by the reaction of the German ethnographer Leo Frobenius on coming into contact with Ife art in 1900. Frobenius was so amazed by the Ife heads, that he came to the rather erroneous conclusion that they could not be the products of natives of the ancient city of Ile-Ife. Ife art compared favourably with the best of Graeco-Roman and Western art. It is, however, to the credit of Frobenius that, despite his misgivings, he did draw attention to his encounter with a great tradition and the existence of a very high civilization at Ile-Ife.

The Ife people produced bronzes but were also adept with clay. Archaeological excavations have revealed the existence of numerous works of art including ritual pots in stylised forms, terracotta sculptures and naturalistic heads, naturalism itself being a highpoint of Ife artistic achievement. Major highlights of Ife art are the Ife heads, generally in naturalistic style, with prominent noses and eyes, which, unlike Nok, are not incised.

Benin

Benin bronzes are perhaps the best known of all Nigerian artistic masterpieces. Benin was attacked in 1897 by a British military expedition. Much of its art was looted and taken away to foreign countries and as a result much of the best of Benin art is abroad. For many years consistent calls for the return of these priceless works have remained unheeded, but the city's artistic attainments continue until the present day. Guilds of craftsmen as well as beneficiaries of age-long family creative traditions dominate the Benin art corpus, and Benin remains an important tourist centre widely admired for the resilience of its distinguished art traditions.

Benin artworks are characterised by intricate designs. Whilst the majority are in bronze, many others are made of ivory, clay and wood. Benin artists made memorial plaques chronicling kings, queens and noblemen, and rectangular plaques on which they recorded life events. They also made figures which symbolise strength, accomplishment and power. Interestingly, there are similarities in diverse Nigerian cultures which occur despite the multiplicity of language and dialect. Examples include the Ikenga figures of the neighbouring Igbo peoples and the Okegga figures erected by the Igala to record successes and achievements. Other common elements of Benin art are representations of animals used in ablutions, particularly leopards and rams.

The Rise of Contemporary Nigerian Art

While Nok, Igbo-Ukwu, Ife and Benin mark the classical period of Nigerian art, the great creative traditions of the Nigerian peoples continue into and beyond the contact and colonial periods of Nigerian history, so that today traditional Nigerian

Head 12th-15th century
Yoruba, Ife, Nigeria
zinc-brass
The National Commission for
Museums and Monuments, Lagos

art continues to be practised all over the country. Artists continue to produce utilitarian trade goods, ritual art, decorative ornaments and motifs, and a large amount of architectural art including carved doors and panels, house posts, pillars, stools, chairs, thrones, and other edifices linked to status and rank. However, unlike in the past when this art existed alone, there is today what is known as contemporary Nigerian art, sometimes also referred to as modern Nigerian art. This is generally remarkable for its departure from linkages with religious or ritual worship, which constituted an important, but by no means the only element of traditional art. Rather it concerns aesthetics, the expression of ideas and values, and social comment.

The rise of contemporary Nigerian art is generally traced to Chief Aina Onabolu and, much later, to Akinola Lasekan and Chief Akeredolu, each of whom sought and received Western European art training during the 1920s. Aina Onabolu trained at the St John's Wood School in London and the Academie Julian in Paris, returning to Nigeria to practise art in the form and manner of European art. The late art legend Ben Enwonwu went to the Slade School of Art in London in the 1950s, so by the time of Nigeria's independence in 1960 the concept of contemporary or modern Nigerian art was already well developed.

The first contemporary Nigerian artists trained at public and private art schools established first by missionaries and colonial officials and later by successor governments of the post colony. Artists received training in Primary and Secondary schools, universities, polytechnics, and colleges of education among other establishments. The logical consequence of this development was the rise of many art schools, styles, and movements in Nigerian art. The universities became catalysts for the rise and development of various art schools, each with a unique character. Some of the most distinguished are to be found at Ahmadu Bello University, Zaria; the Obafemi Awolowo University, Ile-Ife; the Yaba College of Technology; the Institute of Management and Technology, Enugu; the Auchi Polytechnic; and the Alvan Ikoku College of Education, Owerri.

Queen Mother Head 17th century
Benin, bronze
The National Commission for
Museums and Monuments, Lagos

Far left: Figure of an Ooni
12th-15th century
Yoruba, Ita Yemoo, Ife
zinc-brass
The National Commission for
Museums and Monuments, Lagos

Left: Figure of a Man
14th century
Tada village, Kwara State
tin-bronze
The National Commission for
Museums and Monuments, Lagos

Right: Head of a Queen
12th-15th century
Yoruba, Ita Yemoo, Ife
terracotta
The National Commission for
Museums and Monuments, Lagos

Far right: Ancestor Figure (ekpu)
19th century
Oron, wood
The National Commission for
Museums and Monuments, Lagos

The Rebellion at Zaria

The oldest school of formal art training at tertiary level is the Zaria Art School established in 1959 in the then Nigerian College of Arts, Science and Technology and which later became the Ahmadu Bello University. The establishment of this school was a logical consequence of the great artistic traditions of its immediate location – Zaria being one of the most important areas for Nok terracottas. So extensive were the traditional crafts and arts of the north – including the monumental architecture of Kano, the weaving of Olosora of the old Kabba province and the Abuja pottery – that the establishment of an art school became a sine qua non for historical continuity.

Zaria, however, was to become a watershed in the development of contemporary Nigerian art when what Kojo Fosu calls 'the rebellion' took place at this famous college. This was to influence the theory and practice of Nigerian art from then on[5]. About ten leading members of the then newly formed Zaria Art Society – which included such distinguished artists as Bruce Onobrakpeya, Uche Okeke, Yusuf Grillo, and Demas Nwoko – sought a redefinition of the concept and practice of art in their institution. Embracing the natural synthesis theory of Uche Okeke, the group sought to go back to their roots to, in the words of Ola Oloidi: 'extract all possible cultural tools needed to deflate the dominating and flattering face of colonial parasitism'[6]. In other words, they rejected the wholesale embrace of Western art traditions, and sought to merge Western notions of art with Nigeria's artistic heritage and traditions. They rejected art as taught by their foreign lecturers. Bruce Onobrakpeya, one of the leading products of the Zaria school, is among the artists participating in the *Celebrate!* exhibition. Bruce is a leading pioneer artist of the School and one of the best, and perhaps the most exhibited and well-known members of the Zaria Art Society. In his post graduation days he worked under the eagle eyes of Ben Enwonwu, whose sculpture of HM Queen Elizabeth II, who sat for him, has won international acclaim. Bruce is a versatile artist, painter, muralist, printmaker, and art historian. He has paid special attention to printmaking. Chukueggu, writer of a classic on contemporary Nigerian art, describes him as 'Africa's foremost printmaker'[7].

Bruce has explored and developed various forms and concepts in printmaking, producing linocuts, woodcuts and deep etchings. He has also carried out intense research on techniques which have led to the development of his plastocast and plastograph media. Both plastocast and plastograph are cost-saving devices by which plates already used are transformed into new forms and are subsequently employed in executing new artworks. Onobrakpeya's prints are distinguished by their colour combinations. His works show a remarkable understanding and employment of themes from his native Urhobo folktales, thereby creating a reputation for artistic authenticity which became a major factor during the revolt at the Zaria School. An expert book illustrator, his illustrations have been critical in broadening the appeal of the works of some African writers in English, such as Chinua Achebe's *Things Fall Apart*, Cyprian Ekwensi's *An African Night Entertainment*, and *Sugar Girl* by Kola Onadipo.

Mu'azu Sani, another of the exhibiting artists is a distinguished painter and is also a product of the Zaria School. Mu'azu studied and obtained his qualifications at the Ahmadu Bello University, Zaria, where he has taught for several years. He is very widely exhibited. Many of his works draw their themes from the landscape, environment and culture of the north of Nigeria. Mu'azu experiments with various techniques that produce effects akin to variants of Pointillism and his work is powerful and considered. Mu'azu is a typical example of an artist whose works are culturally rooted and his impact on his students, both in terms of experimentation and of cultural approach, is inestimable. Mu'azu belongs to a generation of Nigerian artists who have brought even greater vibrancy to Nigerian art, and raised art practice and propagation to greater intellectual heights. They can collectively take credit for the elevation of art symposia, seminars, and above all research and publications, and the creation of avenues for critical discourse on the trajectory of art in Nigeria.

Also from the Zaria School is the young artist Samuel Uloko Onyilo, who graduated from Ahmadu Bello University in 1999 and has since then managed a flourishing art studio in Abuja. Specialising in painting, he has exhibited at the French

Mu'azu Sani

Bruce Onobrakpeya

Cultural Centre and participated in several group exhibitions. Using art as a medium for social critique, Uloko ably summarises his dispositions and beliefs when he writes: 'In forms and colours, I try to strive towards order in the cloud of dissonance which is over us.'

The Nsukka School

The teaching of art in schools in Eastern Nigeria, namely Government College, Umuahia, and Hope Waddel College, Calabar, provided the stimulus for the eventual establishment in 1960 of an art school at Nigeria's first autonomous university at Nsukka. This was in itself a significant milestone because unlike several other disciplines taught at the university, many people did not understand why art should be studied as an academic discipline. The department grew under the supervision of expatriate lecturers until the events of the Nigerian crisis of 1966-70 created a new community of scholars streaming into Nsukka from other universities across the country. One of Nsukka's most dramatic gains was Uche Okeke – theorist, poet and lyricist, and an exponent of the primacy of drawing in art. Uche was to revolutionise the Nsukka school curriculum, introducing the ideas of synthesis developed at Zaria. But, above all, he gave Nsukka its identity with his work on Uli Igbo art, a system of body and wall painting using indigenous dyes. Uche took Uli to paper and gave it a linear character that would define its image as an intellectual art form. Some of his students were to follow his example and became exponents of this medium. The Uli Art Movement has become one of the most profound in contemporary Nigerian art.

Nkechi Nwosu-Igbo, one of the artists exhibiting in *Celebrate!*, is one of the brightest of the Nsukka Art School and can be classified as a product of the sixth generation of Nigerian artists, that is, those artists who have taken their degrees since the 1990s. Nkechi originally specialised in painting, but has extensively explored several other forms and media.

Samuel Uloko Onyilo

Nkechi Nwosu-Igbo

Apart from numerous works in mixed media, she has become one of the best exponents of installation art. Two of her installations include *Message in a Bottle* and *Seven Green Bottles Standing on the Wall*, produced in 2003. Nkechi has participated in twelve group exhibitions across the country and made numerous television appearances. She runs the Edge Studio together with another young and prolific artist of the school, Uche Edochie.

The Ife School

Asobele, in a guide to modern Nigerian art and artists, appropriately described the Ife Art School as a 'cultural imperative'[8]. Ife is the spiritual home of the Yoruba people and the parade ground and rallying point for Yoruba art and aesthetics. Ife art first gained recognition in the early 1900s and has been compared with the best of Graeco-Roman art. Ife is reputed for excellence in bronze, wood and ceramics. So it is no surprise, therefore, that the Ife Art School was established to consolidate the artistic genius of a city regarded as the ancestral homeland of the Yoruba. Its distinguishing characteristic is the dialogue and sense of community established between town art practitioners and other artists in the locality. This great respect for interplay between town and gown is a mark of distinction for the contemporary artists of the university. Lamidi Fakeye – a leading artist from the traditional background – was recruited and served the very important role of bringing the positive aspects of Yoruba traditional art into the development of the art curriculum and practice at the university. The vitality of art development led to the establishment of the Ori Olokun Group, which flourished for a while under the late Professor Solomon Irein Wangboje. The Ife School, whose 10th anniversary was recently celebrated nation-wide, is also remarkable for the numerous successes of its students, who are reputed to be the only ones to stage and sustain exhibitions across the country.

Other Schools and Movements

Other notable art schools include the relatively young school at the University of Benin, which like the Obafemi Awolowo University, Ile-Ife, is founded in a city of great historical and cultural traditions. Benin art, internationally the best known of Nigerian art, features great bronze heads, plaques, statuettes, and so on. It is hoped that the school will rise to the highest artistic attainments of its environment. The Yaba College of Technology School of Art, the Auchi Polytechnic School, and schools at the Alvan Ikoku College of Education, the Institute of Management and Technology, Enugu, among others are all important components of the art school movement in Nigeria. To these may be added private schools and institutes that train artists and organise exhibitions and workshops such as the Asele Institute established by Uche Okeke at Nimo, in Anambra State; and the Abayomi Barber School based in Lagos, which

has trained some influential artists and which uses the Center for Cultural Studies of the University of Lagos as its base; and, finally, the Oshogbo School of Art which is both a school and a movement.

The definitions of both school and movement in art in Nigeria are similar to the chicken and egg debate. Is a school of art a product of a movement or is a movement the ideological offshoot of a school's explorations? A forthcoming symposium on Nigerian art which has as its theme, style, school and movement in Nigerian Art, will explore this phenomenon. For now, suffice it to say that, while the Nsukka School has given rise to the famed Uli Movement and Ife to the Ona Movement, Oshogbo seems to have attained art relevance as a movement of artists of common ideological bent – the school arising merely as an adjunct of its mission to reach out and propagate indigenous art. Its embrace by the Goethe Institute has given sustenance to the Oshogbo ideal of teaching and inculcating traditions to other artists. These traditions, which have been erroneously tagged 'primitivism', are no more than the preservation of indigenous forms in Yoruba art which spurn the influence of foreign art genres and idioms.

At this point it is appropriate to introduce an artist whose sculptures adorn this exhibition, Bisi Fakeye, one of Nigeria's greatest sculptors and one of the most prolific. Bisi's work, and to some extent, that of his brother Lamidi, introduce an interesting element in the study of the historical development of Nigerian art. Bisi's art has moved away from the purely traditional form into what we know as contemporary art today. Bisi Fakeye's wood sculptures have in fact evolved with time, growing with contemporary times and absorbing characteristics of modern Nigerian art. Artists like Bisi give support to the view that what we call contemporary Nigerian art today is bilinear in development. One line is represented by artists with formal training in art schools and the other by traditional artists who have undergone transformation from within, producing not the art of local religion or palace mystification, but an art which embraces such indices as proportion, symmetry and aesthetic as primary considerations. They also have an eye on the art market.

Bisi's sculptures are culturally authentic, rooted in Yoruba culture, but include elements of Western and contemporary art idioms. Using traditional art as a platform, artists like Bisi Fakeye have harnessed the benefits of contemporary art to create great artistic synthesis that can no longer be fitted within the narrow confines of traditional art. Conversely, many artists of the formal school with roots in contemporary Western art now reach for traditional motifs and forms to create yet another kind of synthesis. Both these syntheses belong to the contemporary art genre. What is today called Nigeria's contemporary art must be understood as benefiting from these two lines of development.

Finally, we cannot conclude this exposé of participating artists without mention of Fred Archibong, a versatile artist who employs multimedia techniques in his works. He often uses fibreglass in the manufacture of his sculptures and plaques, many of which he has executed for Government agencies and departments, and for commercial and industrial establishments. He also runs a workshop and studio, and has made an immense contribution to the training of several young artists from across the country.

Contemporary Nigerian Art and the Future

Art is one of the oldest professions in Nigeria and has continued to gain in status and attention. The rapid multiplication of art schools and the large number of artists turned out each year from art institutions is indicative of the pride of place of contemporary art not only as an academic discipline, but as a profession capable of holding its own among other professional callings. Unlike in the past, when artists found neither recognition nor space for professional practice, today a manifest revolution has taken place in the provision of public studios and workshops by the National Gallery of Art and other agencies. This is the Gallery's response to the UNESCO programme on the status of the artist which emphasises the provision of a conducive living and working environment for the artist. An average of 60 young professional artists benefit from this facility each year in Lagos, to date the only fully completed workshop. Five other workshops are currently under construction in other parts of the country.

Another interesting feature is the variety of training programmes, seminars and symposia that provide young artists with opportunities for professional improvement. The National Gallery of Art runs regular yearly workshops for artists in collaboration with the Center for African Studies, Ohio State University, under the terms of a Memorandum of Understanding signed in 1998. The regularity of symposia, conferences and colloquia has led to the proliferation of art publications, journals and occasional papers which serve to make up for the paucity of literature on Nigerian and African Art. There is also a vastly improved art market, as the number of indigenous art collectors increase by the day and a large number of foreign visitors continue to acquire Nigerian contemporary art. The rising profile of the artist in Nigeria is a cause for joy, allowing artists to display their creativity in advertising, in the embellishment of public buildings and parks, and through the erection of public monuments and so on.

The role of public and private galleries in the promotion and presentation of Nigerian art is notable. The last ten years have witnessed the establishment of hundreds of galleries – public and private – that provide ample exhibition space for young artists. Most are located in Lagos, the melting point of Nigerian cultural activity, but there are also several high profile galleries elsewhere, for example, in Enugu, Ibadan, Abuja, Kaduna, and Jos. Public galleries established by such institutions as the National Gallery of Art and the National Commission for Museums and Monuments are complemented by several new galleries at universities, polytechnics and colleges of education around the country. These are positive indications of a tangible awareness of the need to grow and to project into the future.

Also notable is the rate at which young artists establish studios of their own. Unlike in the recent past and despite the large number of practising artists, most are able to eke out a living, and a few are extremely successful financially. Beyond this mundane consideration is the true worth of the artist as measured by their ideals, their creative impulses, and the spiritual renewal and social re-affirmation implicit in using art for the benefit of society. An outstanding example of such a practitioner is Chinwe Chukwuogo-Roy, a Nigerian in the Diaspora living and working in the UK. Art has been an outlet for personal expression since her childhood days in Anambra State. Following the Biafran war, Chinwe went to London to study art and settled in England after marriage. Since that time painting, printmaking and sculpture have become the means to communicate deeply held views or to explore areas of interest. One series of paintings, for example, examines the slave trade. Another – *Africa: Past, Present and Future* – celebrates African culture. A third, created especially for the *Celebrate!* exhibition, condemns the removal of Nigerian artistic heritage during the colonial period. She is best-known for her Commonwealth portraits of HM Queen Elizabeth II and HE Chief Emeka Anyoaku which are included in the exhibition.

It is Chinwe's vision and commitment which lie behind the realisation of the *Celebrate!* project. She has worked tirelessly over a number of years to promote African culture – and in particular that of Nigeria – to a Western audience through her paintings, lectures, high-profile media interviews, and more recently through schools education initiatives. She is a founder-member of NIDOE (Nigerians in Diaspora Organisation Europe)[9] and a keen supporter of the ideals of the modern Commonwealth, and was determined to bring about a cultural event for CHOGM which would make a lasting impact. Her recognition of the importance of cultural identity (she wears traditional Akwete at all ceremonial occasions) has resulted in her leading a number of art education projects for young people which give them a voice to express their own individuality. It is intended that the *Celebrate!* education programme which follows this pattern and which complements the exhibition, will be run in schools throughout Nigeria for many years to come and will become an important component of the current renaissance in Nigerian art.

Finally, Nigeria's art is an art of the Commonwealth, an important element of the shared aspirations of a community of united, contented and happy citizens bound together by noble aspirations in which artistic creativity occupies pride of place. The people of the Commonwealth share from ancient times a creative tradition that survives today. When we talk about the art of any Commonwealth country, we talk about their great attainments in ancient and contemporary art. The collective, creative wealth of the Commonwealth from Stonehenge to the Taj Mahal to Kano City Walls, constitutes a common heritage to which we can all proudly lay valid claims: the right to share in the triumph of our creativity. It also reminds us of the need for a Commonwealth Cultural Games, where our artists and other creative people can come together, to further the brotherhood already extended by the political leaders of this great family. Cultural exchanges must take centre stage in Commonwealth relations and scholarship. Books, publications and so on must not be accidental occurrences, they must constitute a vital segment of our Commonwealth brotherhood. The Commonwealth should be home to all of us, an enduring brotherhood, a Commonwealth of sustained creative endeavours, for the common good, our Commonwealth.

References and Notes

1. See Ekpo Eyo, *Two Thousand Years of Nigerian Art*, Ethnographica, London in association with the National Commission for Museums and Monuments, Second Impression 1990, p.156

2. *Ibid.* pp. 206 - 212

3. This is ably illustrated in the posters of the exhibition *Treasures of Ancient Nigeria: Legacy of Two Thousand Years*, The High Museum of Art, Atlanta, Georgia, 1981

4. These opinions have been expressed by several researchers into Nigerian material culture, including Ekpo Eyo among others

5. See Kojo Fosu, *20th Century Art of Africa*, Accra, Ghana: Artists Alliance, p.56

6. See Ola Oloidi, *Zarianism: The Crusading Spirit of a Revolution in Nigeria*, in P.C. Dike and Pat Oyelola, ed, *The Zaria Art Society: A New Consciousness*, National Gallery of Art, Nigeria, 1998, p.37

7. See Chinedu Chris Chukueggu, *Contemporary Nigerian Art and Its Classifications*, Virochy International Press, Port Harcourt, 1988, p.111

8. See S.J. Timothy Asobele, *Contemporary Nigerian Art and Artists: A Modern Guide*, Upper Standard Publications, 1992, p.15

9. See www.nidoeurope.org

Ekpo Face Mask 20th century
Ibibio, wood
The National Commission for
Museums and Monuments, Lagos

THE ARTISTS

by John Sheeran

Chinwe Chukwuogo-Roy
drawing at a palm tapper's village
in Benue State, Nigeria

CHINWE CHUKWUOGO-ROY

Chinwe Chukwuogo-Roy was born in Awka, Anambra State, Nigeria, and moved to the UK in 1975, taking up painting as a profession in 1988. Much of her work is in pastels and oils, and her subjects range from portraiture, still life and landscape, to pictures which capture the traditions and cultures of the African continent. She lives and has her studio in Suffolk, UK.

Chinwe has exhibited widely and her work is represented in public and private collections in France, Grenada, Kenya, Malaysia, Mozambique, Nigeria, South Africa, Spain, Swaziland, UK, and the USA.

She received widespread recognition in 2002 for her Golden Jubilee portrait of Her Majesty Queen Elizabeth II, Head of The Commonwealth. Chinwe has won many awards and has featured prominently in the international media, both for her art and also for her charitable and educational work with young people. She was nominated for *Woman of the Year* in the UK and was recently awarded an Honorary Degree of Letters by the University of East Anglia. She personifies the positive aspects both of the Commonwealth and of Nigeria. Her considerable achievements have led her to be widely regarded as a role-model for many black people worldwide.

Cat.17

Her Majesty Queen Elizabeth II 2002

This portrait of Her Majesty Queen Elizabeth II, Head of The Commonwealth, was specially commissioned by the Commonwealth to mark the Golden Jubilee. It was unveiled at the Commonwealth's headquarters at Marlborough House, London, on Commonwealth Day, 11 March 2002, and is being exhibited for the first time in Africa. It is usually on permanent display at Marlborough House.

This picture is among the most vibrant and colourful of the numerous official portraits of The Queen which have been painted during the 50 years of her reign. The portrait imaginatively combines some of the traditional trappings of formal royal portraiture (curtain, chair, Garter robes, dais, balcony, and a commanding full-length pose) with an exciting and innovative multi-image and multi-cultural background. The Queen is viewed refreshingly from an African aesthetic, rather than a Western one, which is characterised by an unmistakable celebratory spirit and a supremacy of hot colours.

The full-length portrait shows The Queen standing at the window of a room in Buckingham Palace. Beyond the balcony is a composite view of some of the best-known sights in the Commonwealth: The Sydney Opera House, Australia; the Houses of Parliament in the UK; the Taj Mahal, India; Great Zimbabwe and Victoria Falls, Zimbabwe; the Kourion Amphitheatre, Cyprus; Montego Bay, Jamaica; the Kasubi Tombs, Uganda; King Njoya's Palace in the ancient Kingdom of Bamun, Cameroon; a First Nations totem pole from British Columbia, Canada; and the Petronas Towers in Kuala Lumpur, Malaysia.

Chinwe was granted five sittings with The Queen at Buckingham Palace in May and June 2001. On completing the portrait in January 2002 she commented: 'The Queen is a great communicator. She's observant, humorous, interesting, and generous with her time. I hope I have succeeded in capturing some of these qualities in my painting. I also wanted to refer to the past and the present, and to show that the strength of the Commonwealth lies in its cultural diversity. I decided the best way was to show different places, buildings and monuments united in an imaginary panorama.'

Study No.1 for Her Majesty Queen Elizabeth II 2001

This lively pastel drawing for the Golden Jubilee portrait was made during the artist's first sitting with The Queen at Buckingham Palace, London on 2 May 2001. The study establishes the composition, pose and dress of The Queen for the official portrait. The drawing records the effects of bright summer light shining through a window on the left, and it provided the artist with her first opportunity to produce a quick study of The Queen's facial features.

Cat.16

His Excellency Chief Olusegun Obasanjo, President, The Federal Republic of Nigeria 2003

This portrait was painted by Chinwe in October 2003 in her studio. It shows President Olusegun Obasanjo standing in an imaginary Nigerian scene which combines two different characteristic Nigerian landscapes typifying the country. In the background is Aso Rock, a famous landmark in Abuja, the Nigerian capital city. For Chinwe, it symbolises stability and permanence and is an icon of Nigeria as an ancient land. In front of the rock, the city of Abuja has been replaced by the lush vegetation of a Nigerian tropical forest, which includes palm and banana trees. Chinwe explains: 'It was important for me to show the President in an open landscape, rather than in a palace or government building. He is a farmer and a man of the earth.'

The President is shown in formal silk Agbada robes with brocade decoration. Chinwe chose the striking mauve colours and brocade decoration herself to act as a counterpoint to the green and browns in the rest of the picture. Despite the relaxed pose of the President's figure, he has great presence and authority. The outline of Aso Rock against the sky introduces a sweeping curvilinear line across the picture plane, leading to the President's head, which is highlighted against the hazy backdrop of the rock. The early morning light in the sky touches the clouds giving them a silver lining. 'Clouds are a common enough sight in Nigeria, but in this portrait they are also symbolic of Nigeria's future,' says Chinwe. 'They are moving towards us and represent the problems facing the country. But they have a silver lining. Nigeria needs the silver lining. They are clouds of hope.'

The President stands on a grassy hill top. The full-length pose and the angle of the President's head complement Chinwe's Golden Jubilee portrait of Queen Elizabeth II. 'The portrait will hang to the left of my portrait of the Queen in the *Celebrate!* exhibition and will be its companion piece,' she says. 'The two portraits are similar in many ways, but also different in just as many. It is interesting to compare and contrast them. I wanted them to work well individually but also as a pair. This was quite a challenge. But I also wanted the portrait of the President to represent tradition and modernity combined in one image. He is a contemporary man standing in a timeless Nigerian landscape.'

Cat.50

One Nation 2003

In this painting Chinwe shows people from all parts of Nigeria in a symbolic gathering to represent a country united by the diversity of its cultures. From the top left moving clockwise are a Hausa man (north west), an Igbo woman (east), a Yoruba man (west), an Edo woman (mid west), an Ijaw man (south), a Fulani woman (north east), a Tiv man (middle), and an Ekoi/Ibibio woman (far east). In the centre is a woman who represents Abuja as the personification of all the peoples of Nigeria. She is identified by her head tie which is green (to represent the Nigerian flag). The head tie is fashionable in Nigeria and is used in this painting to signify both individual and collective identity.

Cat.49

His Excellency Chief Emeka Anyaoku 1999

Chinwe was commissioned in 1999 by the Commonwealth Secretariat to paint this official portrait of Chief Emeka Anyaoku, the Commonwealth Secretary-General 1989-2000. Her Majesty Queen Elizabeth II unveiled the portrait on Commonwealth Day, 10 March 2000 – the Chief's final day in office.

Chinwe's work on the portrait commission began with five six-hour sittings at Marlborough House, the headquarters of the Commonwealth Secretariat in London. She produced a series of pencil drawings, followed by two pastels and one oil study. The final portrait was done entirely in Chinwe's studio, where Chief Anyaoku was painted directly from life during a sixth sitting.

The Chief wears traditional Agbada silk robes and is seated on a carved oak chair in the formal setting of his Marlborough House office. The top shelf of the bookcase is filled with the flags of all 54 Commonwealth member states, representing the global responsibility of Chief Anyaoku's office.

Chief Anyaoku's career spans more than three decades of Commonwealth initiatives. Among the many negotiations in which he was directly involved were those leading to the independence of Zimbabwe and Namibia, and the end of apartheid in South Africa. He is currently Chairman of the Nigerian Presidential Advisory Council on International Relations, a Distinguished Fellow of the London School of Economics, International President of the World Wildlife Fund for Nature (WWF), and the President of the Royal Commonwealth Society and Royal Africa Society.

Cat.5

Our Past, Our History 1998

This painting comes from an ongoing series by Chinwe entitled *Africa: Past, Present and Future*. It is a composite image, rather like a lively pictorial storyboard, and is filled with visual references to African history, culture and society. Faces merge with sculptures and symbols to create a dynamic picture united by fluid brushwork and brilliant colour.

In the centre is Chibinda Ilunga, a 16th century prince of the Luba (Congo) who joined all the warring cultures of the region under one kingdom. Surrounding him in clockwise order, starting in the bottom left-hand corner are: a sculpture of a chief of the Niger Delta; Cetshawayo, King of the Zulus, who defeated the British at Isandlwana in 1879; an Oni of Ife, Yoruba rulers of the 12th to 15th centuries (Nigeria); Queen Nzinga of Ngola, who opposed the Portuguese invasion and slave raiding of her country in the late 17th century; a bronze and ivory Oba Benin commemorative head sculpture; Mukaabya Muteesa I Kayiira, the powerful Kabaka who ruled Buganda from 1856 to 1884; Kata-Mbula, the 109th King of the Kuba (Congo) from 1800-1810, who is shown holding a wooden knife of peace; and Antonio Nigrita, Ambassador from the Kingdom of Kongo, who died in Rome in 1608. Elsewhere in the painting can be seen the King of the Ashanti's golden stool, an Akwete Igbo patterned cloth, and a variety of animal symbols popular in many African cultures, including a snake, bird, bull, lizard, and crocodile. Green and orange leaves are representative of abundance.

One of Chinwe's principal reasons for painting this picture was to reveal in a single image the extraordinarily rich culture of the African continent, which stretches back many thousands of years, but of which millions of Africans are largely unaware.

Cat.4

Cat.1

Bolakeja 1994

Chinwe has likened this painting to a poetic self-portrait. The picture is an attempt to express in a single image her feelings in looking back to when she was a young woman growing up in Nigeria. It is about her background, where she has come from, who she is, and her way of life. Chinwe's face merges with the landscape scene to create an image which appears both soothing and disturbing, so reflecting the artist's dual response to her memory – nostaglia and sense of innocence and loss.

In translation, the title of the picture means 'Get down and fight' and refers to the nickname given to the local lorry shown in the background, which people had to fight to get on each day during the rush-hour journey into Lagos.

Flame of the Forest 1999 *(opposite)*

The painting shows a Flame of the Forest tree in full bloom in a Nigerian landscape. A favourite tree of Chinwe's, it flowers from February to May in spectacular fashion. The tree is transformed into a flame of bright orangey-red and its petals carpet the ground. In the Nigerian countryside, the tree often appears as a distinct glowing red feature in a landscape of greens. Chinwe remembers the tree fondly from her childhood. She has recently produced a series of colourful monoprints inspired by the sight, one of which is also in this exhibition (Cat.19).

Cat.6

Ndu Ozo: Procession at Dawn 1995

This picture belongs to a series of eight paintings Chinwe made following the death of her father, Jeluo, Oguguo Chukwuogo, and the grand funeral which was held in his honour. It shows a group of Ozo men, highly respected figures in Igbo society, leading the funeral procession at dawn. Wearing traditional robes, they carry elephant tusks which are blown like horns to announce their arrival. Chinwe's father was a member of this distinguished group. A notable businessman and landowner, he fought hard for the rights of Nigerians to establish and run their own businesses during the last years of British colonial rule.

Cat.2

Ichi Ozo 1996 *(opposite)*

This print shows a scene from one of the traditional ceremonies marking the funeral of Chinwe's father, Jeluo, Oguguo Chukwuogo. The artist's oldest brother is being handed his father's Ofo (staff) and Alo (cap) to represent his father as an Ozo man.

Cat.3

Chinwe

Agbogho Na Ikolo Mmaw 2000

The four paintings from Chinwe's *Masquerades* series are part of a larger body of work looking at traditional cultures throughout Africa. The masquerade paintings focus on one of the most exciting and expressive features of Chinwe's own native Igbo culture. The pictures are characterised by gestural paintwork and vibrant colours and clearly reflect Chinwe's strong interest in this aspect of her culture which has survived Western influences. Her excitement about the masquerades is as strong now as when she witnessed them as a child.

The two masks in this picture feature a female and male, representing beauty and the beast. Chinwe shows the masks only, with coloured raffia streaking out of them like plumes of colour. The vibrant setting is suggestive of brilliant sunshine, heat and a festive atmosphere. The expressive decoration of the two wooden masks, placed close together, is starkly contrasted. The male mask, on the right, is crudely cut, boldly decorated, and aggressive in appearance. The female mask, by comparison, has a gentle, serene face and seems delicate and fragile – the Igbo ideal of female beauty.

Cat.8

Anumpi 2000

The masquerade combines spiritual ceremony with exuberant entertainment, and embodies the fusion of the spiritual and human worlds. Each masquerade is a personification of a spirit from the after-life or the other world. Each is associated with a particular festival or ceremony and possesses distinctive attributes such as warrior-like prowess, mystical power, youthfulness, or old age. The spirits are covered from head to toe in clothing, raffia and decorative objects, and usually specialise in one or more skills, such as dancing or acrobatics.

The masquerade depicted here is specially reserved as a symbol of respect and honour for entertaining dignitaries and for mourning the dead. Chinwe first remembers seeing the figure when she was a child. It made a deep impression. For this painting, she referred to an old black and white photograph and used her memory and imagination. The superbly expressive and colourful mask is topped by carved wooden double horns set on a small base. The decoration of the mask is carried out by men using natural earth colours, including white chalk. The bright, hot colours Chinwe has used help to emphasise the dramatic intensity of the black shapes and line.

Cat.9

Ifeoma Ataa 2001

After the Ijele masquerade, this is one of the most colourful
and magnificent in Igbo culture. Chinwe saw the figure in
Awka in December 1999, from the upstairs of her house. She
had only ever seen it once before, as it only appears as a mark
of great honour when a very prominent figure in Igbo society
dies. Entire villages will turn out to see it as it dances outside
like a rainbow in movement hovering just above the ground.
The costume is made from many traditional materials. As it
swirls around, mirrors, beads, and carved sculptures catch the
light and make sounds.

Chinwe comments: 'It is frowned upon to draw or take
photographs of some masquerades. After all, it is a special
symbolic event and it would be seen as an insult. So I looked
on and tried to commit as much as I could to memory. I also
studied masquerade dresses in museums. In my paintings, I
haven't been tied down by the necessity for descriptive detail.
It's the explosion of movement and colour that I wanted to get
across, and the remarkable haunting presence of the figures and
masks themselves.'

Cat.10

Nwa Ekpo 2001

The painting shows a children's masquerade which dances and chases, entertaining with its comic gestures. Children watching the masquerade believe it is a spirit which has appeared to both frighten and amuse them with exciting actions and movement. The figure is dressed overall in cloth and wears a wooden mask, so that no part of its body is exposed.

Chinwe comments: 'Masquerades have been a part of my life for as long as I can remember. They have been part of the key events which have shaped my life and have always been there. I can still recall the feverish excitement of watching masquerades when I was a little girl. It was like going to the circus to be entertained or suddenly being taken off to a magical world. My imagination ran wild. I remember being told that the masquerade spirits came from the earth, out of anthills, and I used to think that if I waited by an anthill long enough I would see them coming and going!'

Cat.11

Cat.12

Cleaning the Catch 2001 *(opposite)*

The Catch 2001

The four colour etchings of fishermen going about their daily work are based on rapid drawings Chinwe made of fishermen at Inhambane in Mozambique. She admired their relaxed, down-to-earth approach to their chores, such as pulling the boats in, cleaning their catch, or mending their boats. The men carry their catch over their shoulders or in bags which are not big enough to cover the fish.

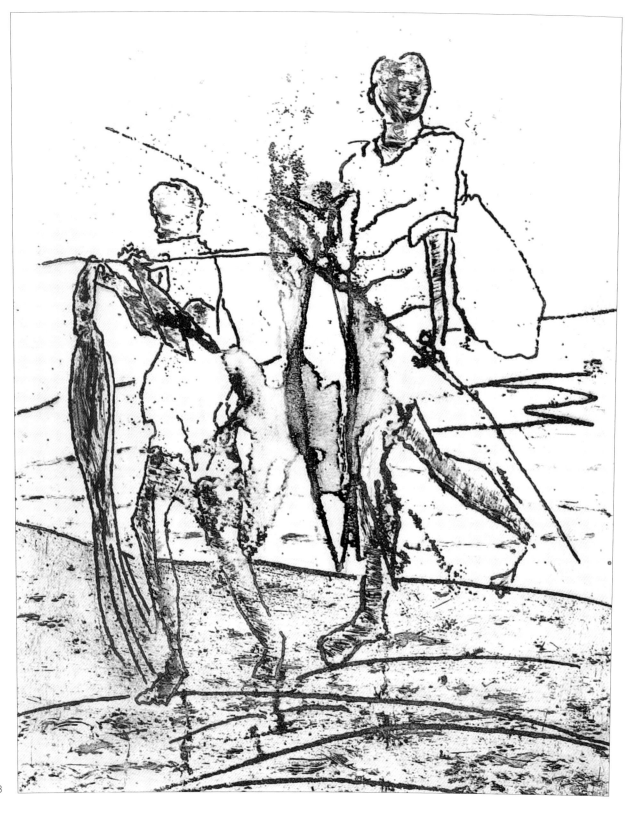

Cat.13

Pulling in the Boat 2001

Cat.14

Mending the Boat 2001

Cat.7

Inhambane Market 2000

Chinwe has spent many hours observing and sketching in a market in the town of Inhambane in Mozambique, which she has often visited on holiday. This is an everyday scene of women with their children, surrounded by fruit and vegetables, and enjoying the shade afforded by the trees. Chinwe is especially interested in the dappled light playing over the figures, the bleaching effect of the intense sunlight in the background, and in rendering the textures of cloth, skin, wood, leaf, and the agricultural produce (which seems to glow as it is illuminated by strong light).

Inhambane Market V 2003

Mama 2002

This is a portrait drawing of Chinwe's mother, who sat for it in the artist's studio.

Cat.22

Self Portrait 2002

Chinwe has produced a number of self-portraits during her career. This is her latest and was drawn from her reflection in a mirror in her studio.

Iru 2002

Iru is Chinwe's baby daughter. This delightful pastel study was drawn from life.

Cat.20

Hibiscus VI 2003
The brilliant colours of the hibiscus flower are a common sight in many parts of Nigeria. The hibiscus is admired for its beauty and is used as a medicinal and health food product.

Cat.25

Hibiscus VII 2003

Cat.26

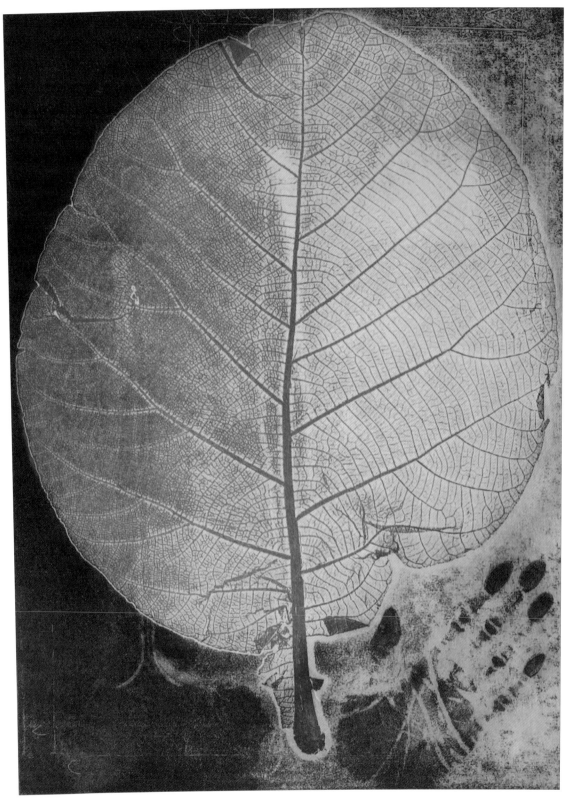

Cat.27

Tree of Life 2003

The symbolism of trees is characteristic of many of the world's cultures and religions. Tree spirits, sacred trees and prophetic trees are well known in spiritual and folk beliefs worldwide. Trees have also provided mankind with building materials, tools, food, and medicines. They are, of course, crucial for the supply of oxygen and in maintaining a balanced climate.

This image juxtaposes the beautiful and delicate image of a single leaf with the artist's hand-print. Chinwe draws parallels between the symbolism of a leaf as the basis of life and her palm print as a mark of human life.

Tree of Life II 2003

Chinwe juxtaposes a leaf with the outline of a head. Just as the head is the symbol of a person and of individual life, so the leaf is a symbol of the life of a tree and its well-being. Both man and nature are interdependent.

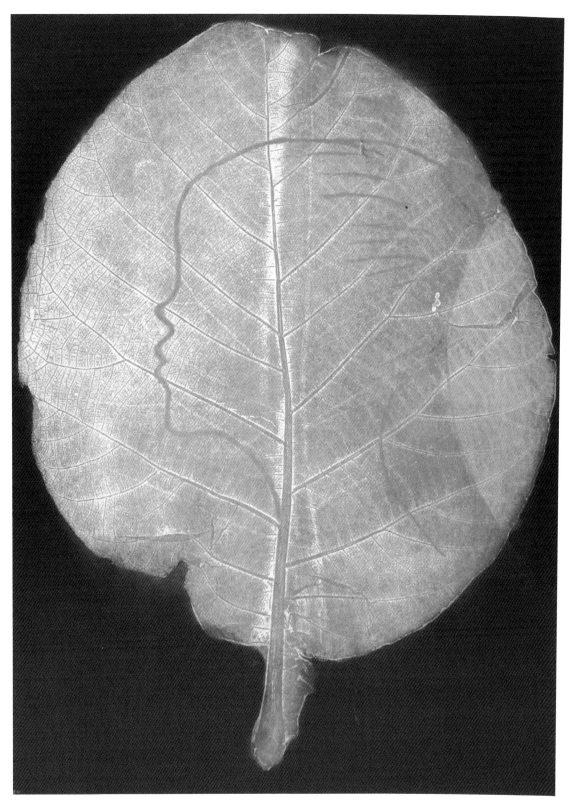

Cat.28

Hidden Treasures, Geneva II 2003

Chinwe's *Hidden Treasures* series of monoprints symbolise the loss of Africa's heritage to Western cities and museums. In each picture a well-known historical African artwork is shown against the backdrop of a Western city. The object seems suspended above the city, more prominent than famous Western buildings and tourist sights. Here a 13th-14th century terracotta head portraying a dead royal personage from the Nigerian Kingdom of Ife now in the collection of the Musée Barbier-Mueller in Geneva is shown against the famous Jet d'Eau fountain and lake in Geneva.

Cat.33

Hidden Treasures, Paris I 2003

The Mumuye wooden standing figure depicted in this print is in a private collection in Paris. The IM Pei Pyramid at the Louvre and the Eiffel Tower are two of the best-known sights of Paris.

The Mumuye people sometimes used figures for divination and healing, to signify the status of elders and to serve as house guardians. The figures are characterised by elongation of the body, ribbon-like arms, and squat, angular legs.

Cat.34

Hidden Treasures, London I 2003

The brass head featured in this picture is the well-known Queen Mother's head from the collection of the British Museum. It is shown against a London backdrop of Trafalgar Square with Nelson's Column and the National Gallery easily recognisable.

The queen shown is Idia, mother of Oba Esigie, the King of Benin from the late 15th to the early 16th century. The head was made to put on her altar after her death in honour of her military and ritual powers.

Cat.35

Hidden Treasures, New York I 2003

The sculpted head shown here is an outstanding Benin ivory mask in the collection of the Metropolitan Museum of Art, New York. To its right is the Statue of Liberty and below is the Manhattan skyline, New York.

The pendant mask is thought to have been made in the early 16th century for Oba Esigie, the King of Benin, to honour his mother, Idia. The king may have worn it at ceremonies commemorating his mother. Today such pendants are worn at annual ceremonies of spiritual renewal and purification.

Cat. 36

Cat.30   Cat.31

Mother and Child I, II and III 2003

These images come from a series of colour lithographs inspired by the extraordinary ancient wall paintings of the Tassili Plateau caves in the Sahara showing hunting scenes and the elegant forms of mothers and children. They were made about 10,000 years ago and discovered in 1956. Chinwe chose images from the wall paintings of a mother and child and produced variations on this theme. She changed the shapes and proportions of the figures to make them more realistic and contemporary. She has also emphasised the intensity of the heat, light and fiery colours. 'I use yellows and ochres to fix my image in the

past,' she explains. 'You can see that the mother and child relationship has not changed over the millennia. The similarity between the distant past and today is striking. The relationship is constant. This is what the *Mother and Child* series is about.'

No More Bloody Wars II 2003 *(opposite)*
Chinwe experienced the horror of war during her childhood and witnessed the devastating effects it can have on a community, family and individual. In this terrifying scene she depicts a young girl fleeing from explosions which have blown up her family and friends, some of whom can be seen dead or injured on the ground. A figure can be seen behind the shell-burst on the left with its hands raised in shock and horror. The gesture is similar to that of *The Scream* by the Norwegian artist Edvard Munch, a reproduction of which hangs in the artist's studio. Chinwe's picture is a damning commentary of the impact and human cost of conflict and war.

Cat.29

Winter Dreams IV 2003
In this monoprint Chinwe visualises herself dreaming of Nigeria in summer during an English winter – its land, sky, flame trees, and houses, and its heat and light. All is a riot of colour and, of course, that much desired element, heat.

82 *Celebrate!* CHINWE CHUKWUOGO-ROY

Flame of the Forest 2002 *(opposite)*

This monoprint relates to an oil painting in the exhibition of the same subject (see Cat.6) showing a flowering tree in a Nigerian landscape. It is one of a series of three monoprints the artist produced at the Limberhurst Press studio in the UK and was painted from memory and imagination directly on to a silk screen, from which it was then impressed on to a sheet of paper.

Nwiru: When the Flame of the Forest Blooms 2003

This painting movingly expresses Chinwe's intense grief about the death of her sister Nwiru in 2001. Chinwe explains: 'Nwiru's life ended tragically during childbirth. After her death, I went to Enugu, where she lived. The Flame of the Forest trees were in bloom. There is a fine bronze sculpture of a drummer on a roundabout as you approach the town. I saw it again and again. It was like an insistent presence. It was intrusive and is forever associated in my mind with what was going on at the time.' Chinwe adopted her sister's surviving baby, Iru, who is shown in the painting.

The following poem by Chinwe complements the picture.

These arms that yearned
To hold my baby
Will yearn forever
Six years of heartache
And pain
Nine months of ecstasy
And labour
Just one jab
One split second
One quick sleight of hand
One tiny prick of a needle
To end my world
My dreams

My anticipated joys of
Mother and child
Don't weep my mother
Don't weep my father
My baby's cry will dry
Your tears
Her laughter will bring joy to
Your hearts
Think of me when
The Flame of the Forest blooms

Cat.48

Cat.43

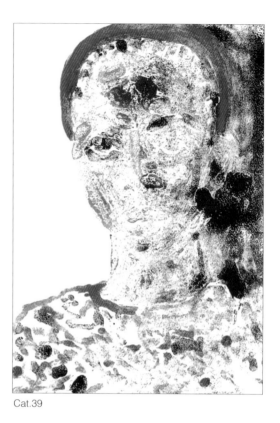

Cat.39

From the Spirit to the Self I-IX 2003

This series of self-portrait monoprints was produced by Chinwe at the Sudbourne Printmakers Group studio in the UK. Chinwe comments: 'I wanted to show through this series of prints that you have to understand your own spiritual self in order to be a fully realised human being. So many people live their lives without a sense of balance between the material and the spiritual. The series shows a gradual transition from the spiritual, represented by the faint and indeterminate head, through to the more fully formed head, which has more colour and character.'

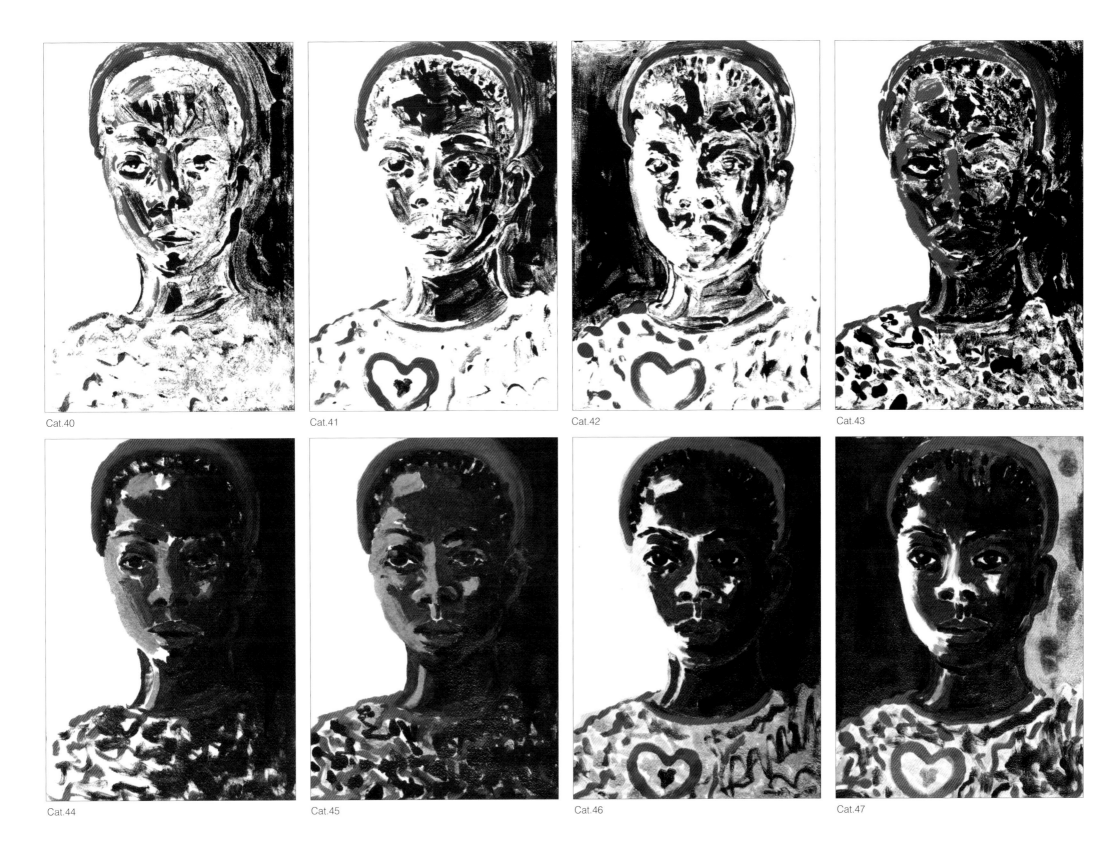

Cat.40

Cat.41

Cat.42

Cat.43

Cat.44

Cat.45

Cat.46

Cat.47

MU'AZU MOHAMMED SANI

Mu'azu Sani was born in Katsina, Nigeria, in 1959. He studied at the Department of Fine Arts at the Ahmadu Bello University, Zaria, where he has worked since 1984 as a lecturer in Painting, Drawing and Basic Design. He has had six solo exhibitions, the most recent being *Mu'azu at 40* in 1999. He has won various awards, including the Joe Adeka prize for the best final year student in drawing when he was at university, and the Merit Award for Outstanding Work in the Guinness Arts Exhibition in Lagos in 1994. In 1992, he was one of 11 African artists selected to participate in a major exhibition of art from non-European countries in Kassel, Germany. In 2000, he was included in the exhibition *Accident & Design* at the Brunei Gallery of the School of Oriental and African Studies at the University of London.

Mu'azu Sani has worked on many commissions including the *Fulani Milk Maiden* mosaic at Kano (1983); the *Golden-Jubilee Impression* for the Friends of the Zaria Leprosy Center (1986); the *Malam and the Almajiris* mural painting in Zaria (1990), and the *Northern Knot* mural in Zaria (1998-9). He is a member of the Society of Nigerian Artists and the Nogh-Nogh Art Group, which is based in Zaria and of which he is currently President. Although best known for his paintings, he also produces collages and sculptures.

'I first started experimenting with the possibilities of liquidised splashing and sprinkling painting techniques in the early 1980s,' he says. 'I wanted to achieve three-dimensional effects of form, space and depth within a composition using a technique which is difficult to control but which can lead to pictures which are very exciting visually. I have been greatly inspired by the Hausa Fulani tradition and have used it for themes and motifs for my own artistic expression. At the moment I am undertaking an in-depth study of the entire Hausa Fulani culture, especially the Sallah celebration (Durbar) in Katsina, Kano, Maiduguri, Sokoto, and Zaria. This is reflected in my current work, but I am also interested in what is happening in Nigeria day-to-day and around the world in general.'

Cat.51

Vision of Hope 1997

This painting was conceived as an abstract symbol of a vision of hope for the future of Nigeria. It shows a barrier of vertical and horizontal stripes of colour with a spinning light approaching from beyond. The swirling circular movement of the pulse of light is contrasted to the rectilinear structure of the barrier, which has the appearance of pieces of torn fabric. Mu'azu Sani comments: 'Political vision has to be good to achieve stability in Nigeria. In this work a messier is steering towards the future into cobwebs of uncertainty and cobwebs of hope. It is steering for a solution to a better Nigeria.'

Bliss After the Year 2010 1997

At first glance this picture seems to show explosive forces and energy in the night sky. Dark and light areas and cold and hot colours are contrasted to heighten the drama of the scene. Amidst the maelstrom, a glimpse is given of a peaceful scene in which a group of people are having a meal, perhaps a picnic, with a car parked in the background. The artist explains: 'It is a commentary about Nigerian vision. The country has had visions which have failed repeatedly. It is hoped that if a fantastic vision for our future can be pursued with all sincerity, then Nigerians will be happy and have all the bliss by the year 2010, which is hinted at in this picture.'

Cat.52

Chuwa Chuwa Boy 1997

This splash picture shows the figure of a boy whose features are being absorbed by sickly-coloured gases. The boy's face and arm have mustard blemishes giving the impression that he is poisoned. Ma'uzu Sani painted the picture in 1997 at a time when toxic fuels were being sold by children in the country because of fuel scarcity. He recalls: 'You would see under-age boys hawking fuel along our roads and most of the time selling bad, mostly poisonous, fuel to motorists. This was a dangerous business and many lost their lives. In this painting a child is depicted with kwashiorkor (a form of malnutrition) after inhaling bad fumes from a passing car for which sadly he was responsible.'

Cat.53

No Peace II 1999

This painting is about the dreadful impact of political instability in the West Africa sub-region. The artist boldly states: 'It shows the state of children in an environment in which warfare consumes innocent citizens. Unless the problem is genuinely addressed, then there will be no real peace in the region and many more children will suffer the same fate.'

The Man, the Camel I 1999

This picture of a man mounted on a camel typifies Mu'azu's painting technique and style, which is both impressionistic and expressionistic. He has studied carefully the way light falls off form and how colours are reflected from object to object, and how both light and colour can unify a scene. The splashing and dripping of paint, though appearing to be uncontrolled and accidental, is highly sophisticated and the result of years of practice. The distinctive style livens up the entire picture surface and the eye is continually put to work when looking at such a picture. The painting is both abstract and figurative. The composition is finely poised. Even the shadows of the man and the camel's head and neck are made interesting to look at. Like the rest of the picture, they swim with intermingled colours and are alive with restless movement.

Cat.55

Warriors of Borno II 1998

A group of mounted warriors are shown in their traditional dress, with spears held erect. An intense light glints off their spears, as well as bleaching the colours and dissolving the forms and features of the horses and men. The artist successfully balances the exotic appearance of the horsemen and the dignity of their bearing, with a wonderfully delicate design and tonal colour scheme, so that both the abstract and figurative possibilities of the subject are explored and maximised for the benefit of the spectator.

Cat.57

THE DURBAR

The Nigerian Durbar festival dates back hundreds of years to the time when the Emirate (state) in the north used horses in warfare. During this period, each town, district, and nobility household was expected to contribute a regiment to the defence of the Emirate. Once or twice a year, the Emirate military chiefs invited the various regiments for a Durbar (military parade) for the Emir and his chiefs. During the parade, regiments would showcase their horsemanship, their preparedness for war, and their loyalty to the Emirate. Today, Durbar has become a festival celebrated in honour of visiting Heads of State and at the culmination of the two great Muslim festivals, Idel Fitri (commemorating the end of the holy month of Ramadan) and Ide-el Kabir (commemorating Prophet Ibrahim sacrificing a ram instead of his son). Of all the modern day Durbar festivals, Katsina Durbar is the most magnificent and spectacular. Id-el-Kabir, or Sallah Day, in Katsina begins with prayers outside town, followed by processions of horsemen to the public square in front of the Emir's palace, where each village group, district, and noble house take their assigned place. Last to arrive is the Emir and his splendid retinue; they take up their place in front of the palace to receive the jahi, or homage, of their subjects.

The festival begins with each group racing across the square at full gallop, swords glinting in the sun. They pass just a few feet away from the Emir, then stop abruptly to salute him with raised swords. The last and most fierce riders are the Emir's household and regimental guards, the Dogari. After the celebrations, the Emir and his chiefs retire to the palace, and enjoyment of the occasion reigns. This fanfare is intensified by drumming, dancing and singing, with small bands of Fulanis performing shadi, a fascinating sideshow to behold.

(description from www.nigeria.gov.ng/culture/touristsites)

Angry Guards 2001
This painting was inspired by the Zazzau Royal Guards at the Emir's Palace in Zaria, northern Nigeria. It is one of a series of pictures the artist has made which document different aspects of traditional Durbar celebrations. In this case, the artist has picked up on the posture and gesture of mounted guards who can appear serious and threatening when there are too many people around the Palace and the Emir is out and about for the celebrations.

Market Woman 2001

This picture shows a woman seated on the ground with baskets of produce which she has brought to a market to sell. It was inspired by the artist's admiration for Nigerian women, who sacrifice and suffer to meet the needs of their families. 'It's about how much our local women have to put up with in order to scrape an existence,' explains Mu'azu Sani. 'They bear children, cook for the family, and go to the markets. This work is a symbol of women's struggle to keep their marriages intact and alive, often by taking on the role of bread-winner.'

BISI FAKEYE

Bisi Fakeye is one of Nigeria's finest sculptors. He was born in 1942 into a family of wood carvers in Ila-Orangun, Osun State, Nigeria and started carving at the age of 10. In the early 1960s he worked under his uncle Lamidi Fakeye at the Catholic Mission in Ondo, and then studied at the Ife Divisional Teacher Training College. His sculptures were first exhibited by the American Society for African Culture (AMSAC) in Lagos in 1963. After exhibitions at the Goethe Institute in Lagos in 1969 and 1971, he was invited as a guest artist to work in West Germany in 1976. He participated in the *Offering to the Gods* exhibition, organised in 1985 by the Society for Nigerian Artists (SNA) at the National Arts Theatre, Iganmu, Lagos. He also exhibited at the Italian Cultural Institute, Lagos, in 1987 and had a solo exhibition entitled *Past, Present and Future* at the German Cultural Institute, Victoria Island, Lagos. In 1989 he was a resident artist with Wajumba in San Francisco, USA, and was also selected for an exhibition of work by leading contemporary Nigerian artists to tour cities in West Germany. He has been a very active member of the Society of Nigerian Artists, serving as its Vice-Chairman and National Treasurer.

Bisi Fakeye has received numerous prestigious commissions. These have included many carved doors for notable buildings, including the Nigerian Embassy in Rome; the Federal Guest House in Victoria Island, Lagos; the Chapel of Christ Our Light, University of Lagos; the Holy Trinity Anglican Church, Ikoto, Ijebu-Ode, Ogun State; and the Chapel of the Healing Cross, Idi-Araba, Lagos. His work is well represented in the National Gallery of Nigerian Art at the National Arts Theatre, Lagos (including a metal gate for the Aina Onabolu Building).

Bisi Fakeye has commented: 'God is the first artist for he created all that is created. Art is all about life and living. I believe creativity is an endless journey for any artist to walk in the passage of life. God is yesterday, today and tomorrow. Art is the past, the present and the future. I hope my work will stand the test of time.'

Cat.59

Germination 2000

'This sculpture came from thinking on a broad base. I realise that plants and animals have a similar way of regeneration. A fertilized seed opens up with the two leaves and the terminal bud in the centre, while with animals, the male and the female have to be present for regeneration to take place.'

Town Crier 2003

'Looking back to the 1950s I remember seeing town criers being used in traditional settings to deseminate information to the community from the Oba (King) and the High Chiefs. This piece is inspired by those memories.'

Cat.60

Cat.61

Adura Longba Agbara Ki Gba (God Answers Only Prayers) 2003
'This sculpture is all about the need for prayer to overcome the problems and long-suffering of Man, rather than the need for power.'

Cat.62

BRUCE ONOBRAKPEYA

Bruce Onobrakpeya is one of Africa's best known and most highly respected artists. A Nigerian Urhobo printmaker, painter and sculptor, he has been described as a 'living legend' who was 'responsible for the renaissance in contemporary art in Nigeria'. He is acknowledged as being one of the leading printmakers in the world and is credited with significant advances in printmaking techniques. In the early 1960s, he was a leading member of the 'Zaria Rebels' who changed the course of art in Nigeria away from a reliance on European concepts and practice towards a distinctly African aesthetic. The fusion of his training in Western techniques and materials with his own heritage and creativity produced an exciting new art which expresses the vitality of Africa's great traditions in a modern style for the contemporary world. He also helped establish the Society of Nigerian Artists in 1964.

Bruce Onobrakpeya was born in Agbarha-Otor, in the Ughelli North Local Government Area of Delta State, Nigeria, in 1932. He studied Fine Art at the Nigerian College of Arts, Science and Technology, Zaria (now Ahmadu Bello University), and graduated in 1961. He taught art at the old Western Boys' High School, Benin City, his *alma mater* Ondo Boys' High School, Ondo; and St. Gregory's College, Lagos, at various times between 1953 and 1980, where he nurtured successive generations of art students, some of whom have themselves grown to become famous names in the field. He has worked as guest teacher and artist-in-residence in Europe and the USA, and has participated in over 60 exhibitions in Nigeria and around the world.

Bruce Onobrakpeya's works are in many international art collections, including the Vatican Museum in Rome, the National Museum for African Art, Smithsonian

Institution, Washington D.C., and the Museum of African and African-American Art and Antiquities, New York. His art is also represented in the collection of Her Majesty Queen Elizabeth II, Head of the Commonwealth, and in the collections of various statesmen and celebrities around the world.

His public commissions range from murals for the Nigerian Independence Exhibition Pavilion (1960) and the Idi-Araba site of the University of Lagos, now College of Medicine (1963), to a design for the 1/6d Nigerian postage stamp in 1970 and glass-etched panels for Murtala Mohammed International Airport, Lagos.

Bruce Onobrakpeya is developing an international art centre that will include a folk museum of art as well as a gallery of contemporary African art in Agbarha-Otor, Delta State. The centre has hosted the Harmattan Workshop series for visual artists since its inception in 1998, initiated and sponsored by Bruce with support from corporate organisations. Created with a vision to provide opportunities for artists to come together to experiment, share ideas and carry out research, the Workshop, which has gained international recognition, is the only such forum in Nigeria where artists of all backgrounds come together for four weeks to engage in artistic and academic projects.

Bruce Onobrakpeya has received numerous prizes and awards, including the British Council Award (1969); the Pope Paul VI Gold Medal for participating in an exhibition to commemorate the Pope's 80th birthday celebrations (1977); the Fulbright-Hays Award (1979); the 5th Triennale-India Silver Medal (1982); the Asele Institute Certificate of Honour (1985); the Solidra Circle Award (1985); an Honorary Degree of Doctor of Letters, University of Ibadan (1989); the Bendel State Merit Award (1990); the Classique Magazine Star Award of Achievement for contributing immensely to society (1990); the Delta State Merit Award for Excellence in Arts (1995); the Masters' Award (1999); the Fellowship Award of the Society of Nigerian Artists (1989); and the Member of the Federal Republic (MFR) National Merit Award (2002).

Cat.68

Ekugbe (Unity) 1995

Ekugbe is an Urhobo word for unity. The artist has described this oil painting as: 'a prayer for the unity of the many different groups in our country to continue to work together for one nation.' The mask represents the divine head or supreme intelligence which holds the people together.

Triumph 1995

The picture was conceived as a divine providence to the suffering masses and is best explained by the following poem:

The Masses are without jobs
And are hungry
They lack basic needs –
Shelter, light, potable water,
Medicine and good roads.
Focus on mineral extraction and wealth
Create environmental problems and discourages farming.
Influx of foreign goods
Close down industries
And devaluate the currency.
Education of the children suffers.
Armed robbery, assassination,
Engineered ethnic strife,
Corruption and the looting of the people's wealth
By their supposed leaders,
All create insecurity and refugee problems
And a new slavery.
The masses pray for divine intervention
And will surely triumph
Over these mortal challenges.

Cat.69

Cat.67

Mother and Child (Omo Voni) 1986

This picture celebrates the cultural revival or black renaissance which is sweeping through Africa in the wake of political independence. The mother and the child mounted on a circular mask are surrounded by figures emerging from a dark background.

Travail of the Continent 1999

This work is inspired by the many human and material disasters which have taken place within the African continent in the last decade of the 20th century. These include the forceful take-over of government, leading to civil wars in Sierra Leone and Liberia; inter-ethnic wars between Tutsi and Hutu; and neo-colonization leading to economic strangulation. The picture is composed of nine masks which are tortured, angry, weeping, and sad. The method of production is painted inverse-etching, called additive plastograph, which has been specially developed by the artist.

Cat.77

Hanging the Ogoni Nine 2001

This picture is a reflection on the death of the nine Ogoni martyrs who died fighting for their fatherland. Bruce Onobrakpeya comments: 'The hanging is positioned at the base of an imaginary colonnade of totems, which wear sad, weeping faces resulting from the alienation of a people whose land flows with black gold.' The picture is a digital-aided drawing with watercolour.

Cat.70

Lament of the Delta 2002

The picture shows an altar of lamenting totems, at the base of which are the shared remains of the victims of the Jesse pipe-line fire disaster which claimed over a thousand lives. The composition is a digital-aided drawing with watercolour.

Cat.74

Cat.71

Bridge Across Time 2002

This is an installation of old and new art works, bone fossils, beads, and discarded mechanical and electronic parts including computer parts and jute fibre. The objects in the composition lead from the fossils and ancient art work of the past to the present computer age and suggest a future of limitless possibilities.

Aerial Landscape 2001 *(opposite)*

This work is an installation of discarded computer parts. The piece is primarily inspired by the view of the land as seen from a plane thousands of feet above the ground. It concerns the beauty which can be found in machines, particularly those parts which are hidden. The work also symbolises the new information technology and energy which can be harnessed for good, but which is also equally dangerous when put to bad use. The picture is also suggestive of the possibility of future life for man in the galaxies.

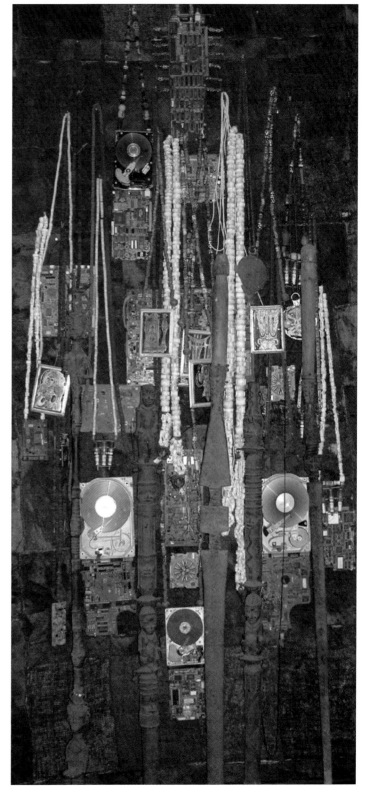

Cat.73

Cat.76

Warring Youths 2003

The picture shows the effect of under-development on the youths of Delta state, which, though rich in mineral wealth, is poor in infrastructure, governance and resource management that can educate and gainfully employ the teaming population of young people. The picture is a digitally-aided drawing with watercolour.

Ekugbe (Unity) VIII 2003 *(opposite)*

This is a metal-foil print which is a study for a larger engraving which has been specially produced for the *Celebrate!* exhibition. The picture is a celebration of Nigerian unity in diversity. The idea for the picture goes back about three decades to the Nigerian civil war, which had threatened the break-up of the country.

Cat.75

NKECHI NWOSU-IGBO

Nkechi Nwosu-Igbo is a painter, poet and conceptual artist. She was born in 1973 and graduated from the Department of Fine and Applied Arts of the University of Nigeria, Nsukka, in 1997. She is a full-time studio artist working and living in Lagos. She has had over 17 solo, joint and group exhibitions in Nigeria, South Africa, Italy, and the USA. Her installations and performances about violence and abuse have aroused controversy both in Nigeria and abroad. She is experimenting with video installation and currently working on a project in which she combines poetry, performance and painting.

In this exhibition, Nkechi presents a collection of paintings from her on-going series entitled *Heart Space*, which has been described as: 'a set of works dealing with those spaces in our heart and psyche that crave wholeness; be they spaces of inadequacy and unfulfilment, insecurity and indirection, or fragmentation and desire.'

Nkechi Nwosu-Igbo comments on her work: 'The challenges I have decidedly subjected myself to over the years have been those of creating exciting art with the barest elements, be it aesthetic or conceptual; and a continuous search for the essence as opposed to creative verbosity. In doing so, my aesthetic expression ranges from paintings and drawings to installations and performances. My themes remain essentially relevant and sensitive to the human condition through social, moral, mental, and economic commentary. In this I find meaning in my very existence. The symbols I use in my work vary from Uli to Nsibidi. Uli is an art form of the body and of wall decorations found among the Ibo people of eastern Nigeria. Nsibidi are sacred symbols used by secret societies of the southern areas of Nigeria for communication.'

I Can Make It 2002

'In this pastel painting the flower is a symbol of hope. I believe that whatever situation you find yourself in, you can believe yourself out of it; it is all in your thinking!'

Cat.78

Dreams 2003

'Dreams portray our search for fulfilment as Nigerians; whether we hope to create spaces in our lives or erase and edit existing spaces, as humans we all crave and dream of better lives.'

Cat.82

Cat.81

Memoirs 2003

'The picture is predominantly in blue colours. It was done during the early stages of my pregnancy when I was always blue and sick. I tried to record everything I felt both in my journal and in my paintings. A lot of the poems and paintings I created then were dark and lonely, depicting my conflicting happiness and the changes I felt in my body.'

My Heart Your Haven 2003

'This mixed media work is a reassurance to my unborn baby that Mama will always be there to fill up any space or to provide any refuge needed.'

Cat.85

SAMUEL ULOKO ONYILO

Samuel Onyilo was born in 1971 in Jos Plateau State and grew up in Benue State, eastern central Nigeria. In the early 1990s he studied at the Ahmadu Bello University, Zaria. He is a member of the Igabo Group of Artists and the Society of Nigerian Artists. His works are on display in the National Assembly of Nigeria, Abuja, and in the Nigerian Embassy in Sweden. In 2002 he completed a mural for the Polo Club in Kaduna, Nigeria, and a solo exhibition called *Innerscape* opened at the French Cultural centre in Abuja in September 2003. Two publications have recently been produced on his work: *Forms and Colours from Contemporary Confusion* by Professor Mac Nze Odu, and *Eroica: A Study of the Art of Samuel Uloko Onyilo Otukpo* by Ngozi Adamu-Ibrahim of the National Gallery of Art, Nigeria. His paintings are to be found in many art collections throughout Nigeria and abroad.

Samuel Onyilo has commented on his work: 'All I try to express is the complexities of my time, a pseudo-materialistic age, a world stripped of its spirituality by inhuman technology. Through forms and colours, I try to strive towards order in the cloud of dissonance and a light of hope in a dark world.'

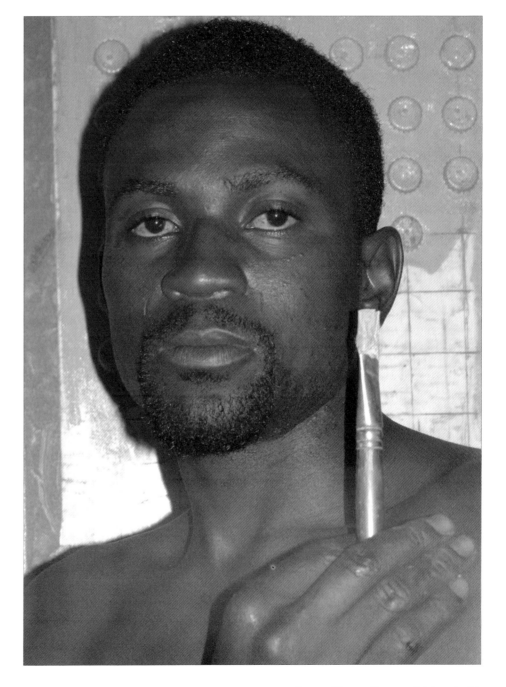

Cat.88

Face (Window to the Mind series) 2003

'My friend said to me, the most difficult task Shakespeare undertook was to try to penetrate the mind through the face. My first fascination with the human face is in the dramatic distribution of light and shade on the different parts. Careful gradation of light and shade; the opposites reappearing once more; the opposites are a path into the depth of man.

Later on, I studied gesture and mood. I saw very vacant faces, old faces, young, rich, poor, beautiful, and ugly faces. Irrespective of their station, each face radiates the state of the owner's mind. Sometimes the face conceals the content of the mind; at other times it gives up the secrets of the mind. The face radiates a charm words will never be able to describe.

It is the enigma of the human face that fascinates me. I have on occasions come close to getting to the secret. I have also fallen prey to the face. Maybe, one day I will conquer the face; maybe the face will conquer me.'

Cat.89

Composite Earth 2003 *(opposite)*

'The raped landscape, the polluted stream and air, the crater left by mining, eroding not only our houses and farms, but the landscape's soul, eat deep into me. Man has refused to see himself as stakeholder in the delicate balance in which we all exist. Life is symbiotic; there is an inter-relationship of all that exists: the land, the sea, the heavens, man and the animals. Our quest for profit has blurred our understanding. We live in a highly artificial and impersonal world. Our actions are the biggest plague and will consume us.

I try to see how I can call this menace to the attention of men of my time; to show also the beauty around us; to see eternity through all that surrounds us. We can encounter in the corn stalk the timeless message that will shape and mould us into the people we ought to be. We must live in harmony with nature.'

Cat.90

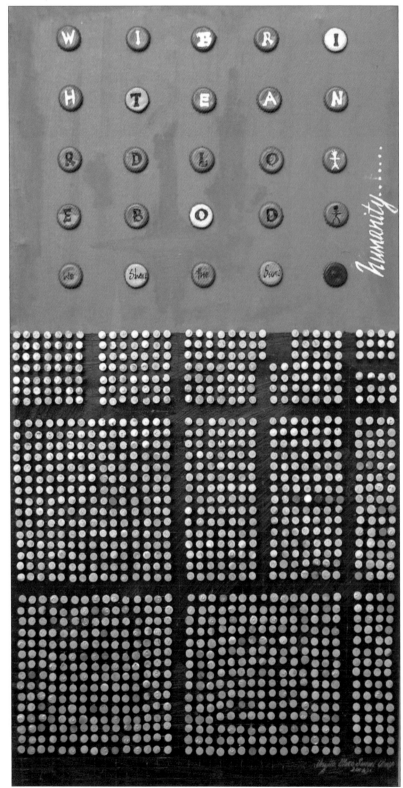

Cat.92

Fidelio 2003

'The decision to start working with bottle tops and nails struck me on a very personal level. There was a growing agitation in me of how to externalise my inner conflicts, the bitter realities I confront persistently, the harsh reality that covers the landscape. Images of pain, cruelty, impoverishment, institutional cruelty, and global moral recession are the chief influences that spur me into this medium of expression.

Sometimes I wonder why it befalls me to see what I see. I realised the pressure and all the social ills I have mentioned are alien to the soul of man.

The contradiction is the fact that I find the ugly idea extremely fulfilling and beautiful. I see and experience the liberating power of pain and get a clearer understanding of the diametrical measure of life.

The bottle tops represent to me the rejected of the earth, the down-trodden, the marginalised. I pick the bottle tops, dress them up and use them in my compositions.

The secularisation of man in our highly materialistic and technological, banal society is not only reductionist but also strips man of his inherent spirituality. I want to show through the bottle tops the extraordinary in all that is seen as ordinary. Each reality we encounter has a trace of divinity imprinted on it. Man ought to be seen in his true nature as not only unique matter but capable of transcendence. People should first be seen as human beings before being subjected to any line of categorisation. We are humans first before we are male or female, Christian or Muslim, white or black.

My work is a call to contemporary man to go back to the cradle; to humanistic values; to restore man to his proper place in creation. The bottle top seals the content of the bottle, but unfortunately the earth is littered as soon as the top is pulled off the bottle. This is the disposable nature man has taken in our money-obsessed society.

The nails are organised carefully in relationship to other elements of the composition. They represent to me pain and passive cruelty organised in such a way that is difficult to discern. Pseudo-policies are sold on a global scale to the world and made to look beautiful at face value. I am very weary of the modern state's quest for economic and military might at the expense of its subjects. The state is so detached from its subjects and mostly never changes its policies based on considerations of justice.

I carefully organise the nails and see through them the complexities of my time; our collective psyche traumatised by activities and policies that are not in harmony with humanistic values. I have had a good dose of rejection, I know and have felt the piercing bites of oppression, but have equally discovered the strength of the human soul over physical challenges. I believe the more inward we go, the more we understand life as a whole. There is need for contemplation and solitude.

On the surface of my pictures there is unification of spirit and elemental matter. In all I do I see a hope; a hope that is rooted and affirmed by the very diametrical structure of life. The beauty of light is felt better in the dark.'

Eroica 2003

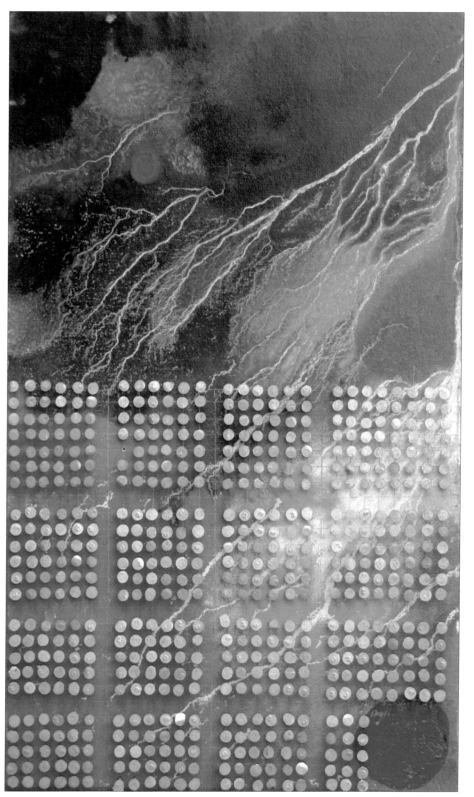

Cat.93

FRED ARCHIBONG

Fred Archibong was born in 1959 in Old Town (Obutong), Calabar, Nigeria, and studied at the Federal Government College, Warri, Nigeria, and at the School of Arts Institute in Illinois, USA. He has exhibited his artworks in many countries, including South Africa and the USA, and is highly successful within the corporate sector. He has received many notable art commissions, for example, from the Nigerian National Assembly, the Nigerian National Petroleum Corporation, and the Nicon Hilton Hotel, Abuja. A recent work for the UNESCO headquarters in Paris was jointly unveiled by Presidents Obasanjo and Chirac. He has also been commissioned to create a sculpture for Nigeria House in New York. He works in many different media, ranging from oil and watercolour to clay and steel.

Fred Archibong has also been appointed to a variety of organisations. He is a Commissioner of the Nigeria Securities and Exchange Commission; Chairman of the Marketing and Publicity Committee of the Nigerian Tourism Development Committee; an Affiliate Business Council Member of the World Tourism Organisation; and an art consultant to the Nigerian Presidency.

Nudity 1980

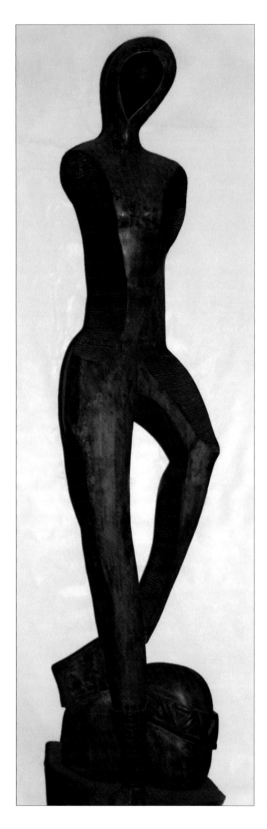

Cat.95

Family Group

Cat.101

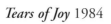

Tears of Joy 1984

Cat.96

Rhythm 1986

Cat.97

Mother Care 2002

Cat. 100

Mask 1999

Cat.98

Cat.99

Cat. 104

Faces 2003

Cat.102

Salamatu, The Fulani Milk Maid 2003

Cat.103

CATALOGUE OF WORKS

CHINWE CHUKWUOGO-ROY

1. *Bolakeja* 1994
   oil on canvas
   49.5 x 35.5 cm

2. *Ndu Ozo: Procession at Dawn* 1995
   oil on canvas board
   40 x 45 cm

3. *Ichi Ozo* 1996
   woodcut
   42.5 x 58.5 cm

4. *Our Past, Our History* 1998
   oil on canvas
   135.5 x 113 cm

5. *His Excellency Chief Emeka Anyaoku* 1999
   oil on canvas
   171 x 127 cm

6. *Flame of the Forest* 1999
   oil on canvas
   65 x 91 cm

7. *Inhambane Market* 2000
   etching and aquatint
   37 x 40 cm

8. *Agbogho Na Ikolo Mmaw* 2000
   oil on canvas
   76 x 61 cm

9. *Anumpi* 2000
   oil on canvas
   76 x 61 cm

10. *Ifeoma Ataa* 2001
    oil on canvas
    76 x 61 cm

11. *Nwa Ekpo* 2001
    oil on canvas
    76 x 61 cm

12. *Cleaning the Catch* 2001
    etching
    28.5 x 41 cm

13. *The Catch* 2001
    etching
    40 x 25.5 cm

14. *Pulling in the Boat* 2001
    etching
    28.5 x 41 cm

15. *Mending the Boat* 2001
    etching
    40 x 25.5 cm

16. *Study No.I for Her Majesty Queen Elizabeth II* 2001
    pastel
    82.5 x 55 cm

17. *Her Majesty Queen Elizabeth II* 2002
    oil on canvas
    183 x 112 cm

18. *Her Majesty Queen Elizabeth II* 2002
    lithograph
    54 x 43 cm

19. *Flame of the Forest* 2002
    monoprint
    75 x 91.5 cm

20. *Self Portrait* 2002
    pastel
    73 x 52.5 cm

21. *Iru* 2002
    pastel
    52 x 44 cm

22. *Mama* 2002
    pastel
    73 x 52.5 cm

23. *Self Portrait V* 2002
    monoprint
    60.5 x 50.5 cm

24. *Family Portrait* 2002
    oil on canvas
    121.5 x 91 cm

25. *Hibiscus VI* 2003
    monoprint
    60.5 x 50.5 cm

26. *Hibiscus VII* 2003
    monoprint
    91.5 x 64.5 cm

27. *Tree of Life* 2003
    etching
    49.5 x 36 cm

28. *Tree of Life II* 2003
    etching
    49.5 x 36 cm

29. *Winter Dreams IV* 2003
    monoprint
    70 x 91.5 cm

30. *Mother and Child I* 2003
    lithograph
    85 x 66.5 cm

31. *Mother and Child II* 2003
    lithograph
    85 x 66.5 cm

32. *Mother and Child III* 2003
    lithograph
    50.5 x 83.5 cm

33. *Hidden Treasures, Geneva II* 2003
    monoprint
    51 x 61 cm

34. *Hidden Treasures, Paris I* 2003
    monoprint
    51 x 61 cm

35. *Hidden Treasures, London I* 2003
    monoprint
    51 x 61 cm

36. *Hidden Treasures, New York I* 2003
    monoprint
    51 x 61 cm

37. *No More Bloody Wars II* 2003
    monoprint
    51 x 61 cm

38. *Inhambane Market V* 2003
    etching
    35.5 x 27 cm

39. *From the Spirit to the Self I* 2003
    monoprint
    41.5 x 29.5 cm

40. *From the Spirit to the Self II* 2003
    monoprint
    41.5 x 29.5 cm

41. *From the Spirit to the Self III* 2003
    monoprint
    41.5 x 29.5 cm

42. *From the Spirit to the Self IV* 2003
    monoprint
    41.5 x 29.5 cm

43. *From the Spirit to the Self V* 2003
    monoprint
    41.5 x 29.5 cm

44. *From the Spirit to the Self VI* 2003
    monoprint
    41.5 x 29.5 cm

45. *From the Spirit to the Self VII* 2003
    monoprint
    41.5 x 29.5 cm

46. *From the Spirit to the Self VIII* 2003
    monoprint
    41.5 x 29.5 cm

47. *From the Spirit to the Self IX* 2003
    monoprint
    41.5 x 29.5 cm

48. *Nwiru: When the Flame of the Forest Blooms* 2003
    oil on canvas
    112 x 81 cm

49. *One Nation* 2003
    oil on canvas
    96 x 75.5 cm

50. *His Excellency Chief Olusegun Obasanjo, President, The Federal Republic of Nigeria* 2003
    oil on canvas
    183 x 112 cm

MU'AZU SANI

51. *Vision of Hope* 1997
    oil on canvas
    80 x 80 cm

52. *Bliss After the Year 2010* 1997
    oil on canvas
    85 x 86 cm

53. *Chuwa Chuwa Boy* 1997
    enamel on canvas
    80 x 80 cm

54. *No Peace II* 1999
    enamel on canvas
    77 x 109 cm

55. *Warriors of Borno II* 1998
    oil on canvas
    80 x 100 cm

56. *The Man, the Camel I* 1999
    enamel on canvas
    80 x 100 cm

57. *Angry Guards* 2001
enamel on canvas
80 x 100 cm

58. *Market Woman* 2001
oil on canvas
77 x 109 cm

BISI FAKEYE

59. *Germination* 2000
cam wood
183cm

60. *Town Crier* 2003
cam wood
94 cm

61. *Adura Longba Agbara Ki Gba : God Answers Only Prayers* 2003
oroo wood
97cm

62. *Hospitality* 2003
ebony wood
77cm

63. *June 12* 2003
cam wood
94 cm

64. *Ireti II: Hope* 2003
ebony wood
190 cm

65. *Ike-Omo: Mother's Love and Care for the Baby* 2003
cam wood
198 cm

66. *Oye Lagba Now: The Sage* 2003
cam wood
42 cm

BRUCE ONOBRAKPEYA

67. *Mother and Child (Omo Voni)* 1986
plastograph
114.5 x 86.5 cm

68. *Ekugbe (Unity)* 1995
oil on canvas
210.5 x 146 cm

69. *Triumph* 1995
oil on canvas
210.5 x 145 cm

70. *Hanging the Ogoni Nine* 2001
drawing and watercolour
121 x 85 cm

71. *Aerial Landscape* 2001
mixed media assemblage
126.5 x 180.5 cm

72. *Rape of the Land* 2001
drawing and watercolour
125 x 94 cm

73. *Bridge Across Time* 2002
mixed media assemblage
214 x 114 cm

74. *Lament of The Delta* 2002
drawing and watercolour
116 x 87 cm

75. *Warring Youths* 2003
drawing and watercolour
122cm x 87 cm

76. *Ekugbe VIII* 2003
metal study for engraving
116 x 169 cm

77. *Travail of the Continent* 1999
plastograph
111 x 85.5 cm

NKECHI NWOSU-IGBO

78. *I Can Make It* 2002
pastel on paper
26 x 22cm

79. *Riding The Storm* 2002-3
acrylic and mixed media on canvas
107 x 84 cm

80. *Dreams of a Fisherman* 2003
pastel on paper
26 x 22cm

81. *Memoirs* 2003
pastel on paper
26 x 22cm

82. *Dreams* 2003
pastel on paper
26 x 22cm

83. *Some Hours to Peace* 2003
pastel on paper
26 x 22 cm

84. *Present Laughter* 2003
pastel on paper
26 x 22 cm

85. *My Heart, Your Haven* 2003
acrylic and mixed media on canvas
107 x 84 cm

86. *Deadlines For My Memories II* 2003
acrylic and mixed media on canvas
107 x 84 cm

87. *Life Interruptions* 2003
acrylic and mixed media on canvas
107 x 84 cm

SAMUEL ULOKO ONYILO

88. *Face (Window on the Mind series)* 2003
pencil
37 x 49 cm

89. *Inscape* 2003
liquidised oil on canvas
92.5 x 61 cm

90. *Impression (Contemplating the Earth)* 2003
liquidised oil on canvas
99 x 99 cm

91. *Composite Earth* 2003
liquified oil on canvas and jute
71 x 101.5 cm

92. *Fidelio* 2003
mixed media including oil paint, nails and bottle tops on canvas on board
90 x 47 cm

93. *Eroica* 2003
mixed media including oil paint and nails on canvas on board
62 x 38 cm

94. *Landscape Within* 2003
oil on canvas
119.5 x 119.5 cm

FRED ARCHIBONG

95. *Nudity* 1980
wood
305 cm

96. *Tears of Joy* 1984
fibreglass
122 cm

97. *Rhythm* 1986
wood
152 cm

98. *Mask* 1999
wood
51 cm

99. *Expression* 2000
polyguard
152 cm

100. *Mother Care* 2002
polyguard

101. *Family Group*
metal
46 cm

102. *Faces* 2003
metal
91.5 cm

103. *Salamatu, The Fulani Milk Maid* 2003
metal
122 cm

104. *Images in Motion* 2003
metal
91.5 cm

105. *Expectation* 2003
telecotate
305 cm

Acknowledgements

Sheeran Lock, the organisers of *Celebrate!*, would like to thank the following for all their help and advice during the preparation of the exhibition and commemorative publication:

Kazeem Abimbola, *MTN Nigeria*

Anthony Adeloye, *Nigeria High Commission Library*

Dr. Yemo Adeniji

Abayomi Adeshida, *photographer*

Omuye Ajibade, *CHOGM Abuja Task Force*

Judith Anyinkwa

Fred Archibong, *artist*

Doug Atfield, *photographer*

Roger Baker, *Suffolk Chamber of Commerce*

Amitav Banerji, *Commonwealth Secretariat*

Linda Barrett, *Qua Tendis*

Marilyn Benjamin, *Commonwealth Secretariat*

Virginia Blackmore, *Qua Tendis*

Anuli Chukwuogo

Cecelia Chukwuogo

Chinwe Chukwuogo-Roy, *artist*

Yinka Craig, *presenter*

Paul Chike Dike, *Nigerian National Gallery of Art*

Ambassador A.O. Esan, *CHOGM Abuja Task Force*

Alex Ewuzie, *Winsor & Newton, Nigeria*

Bisi Fakeye, *artist*

Funmi Fakeye

Norman Finch, *Norman Finch Transport*

Ray Fishwick, *designer*

Teddy Hanmakyugh, *National Television Authority, Nigeria*

Peter Igho, *National Television Authority, Nigeria*

Ayo Ighodaro, *Bishopstone Associates*

Chuks Iloegbunam, *The Vanguard*

Billy Lawson, *LTC Advertising Ltd.*

Joanne Littlejohn, *Sheeran Lock*

Stephen Lock, *editor*

John Middleditch, *Fraser Gallery*

Stuart Mole, *Royal Commonwealth Society*

Fiona Mortimer, *Qua Tendis*

Gilio Moscardini, *Winsor & Newton*

John Mortimer, *Business Link*

Alison Newell, *Sheeran Lock*

F. Ndefo, *Federal Ministry of Education, Nigeria*

A.U. Nwadike, *Federal Government's Boys' College, Nigeria*

Rev. Sister Chidebelu Nwigwe, *Regina Pacis Girls Secondary School*

Nkechi Nwosu-Igbo, *artist*

C. Obioha, *Federal Ministry of Education, Nigeria*

Friday Okai, *Nigerian High Commission, London*

Bruce Onobrakpeya, *artist*

Chris Onyemenam, *Bishopstone Associates Ltd.*

Samuel Uloko Onyilo, *artist*

Brian Pearson, *Suffolk Offset*

Steve Pleune, *Winsor & Newton*

Shobhna Rattansi, *Commonwealth Secretariat*

Roderick Roy, *Qua Tendis*

John Saddington, *Commonwealth Secretariat*

Mu'azu Sani, *artist*

Maryann Ugo, *barrister*

Uche Uwechia, *Qua Tendis*

Ugo Uyah, *CHOGM Abuja Task Force*

Ifeoma Uzoka, *Qua Tendis*

David Wade, *Suffolk Offset*

Sarah Wyke, *editor*

Daniel Zagni, *Suffolk Offset*

The CCJ Cultural Troupe from Benue State, Nigeria, performing in Abuja

The Organisers

John Sheeran

As a director of the creative communications consultancy Sheeran Lock Ltd, John Sheeran has created projects for clients which use art to communicate across cultural and economic boundaries. He has been invited to curate numerous international exhibitions. These have included *Travels with the Prince: The 50th Birthday Art Exhibition of HRH The Prince of Wales* at Hampton Court Palace; *Painting & Patronage*, a unique Anglo-Saudi cultural collaboration; and *Our World in the Year 2000: The United Nations Millennium Art Exhibition*, opened by Kofi Annan at the UN Headquarters, New York. More recently he has created innovative corporate social responsibility art and education programmes which have been praised at Ministerial level as examples of best practice. In 2002 he curated *Chinwe: An Exhibition for The Commonwealth Games* in Manchester.

Dr Paul Chike Dike

Paul Chike Dike was appointed Director of Research and Training at the Nigerian National Commission for Museums and Monuments in 1990; Chief Executive of the Nigerian National Gallery of Art in 1993; and Director-General of the National Gallery of Art in 2000. He has organised several exhibitions of Nigerian art, including at the *Pan-African Festival* in Ghana in 1997 and 1999, and for the *Exhibitions of Countries of the Non-Aligned Movement* in Indonesia in 1995 and in India in 1997. He is a founding-editor of the *Nigerian Journal of Art* and has written articles and books on both traditional and contemporary Nigerian art.

SHEERAN LOCK

Sheeran Lock Ltd was established as a creative communications consultancy in 1990 by John Sheeran, an art curator, and Imogen Lock, an expert in communications. The UK-based company is best known for the innovative and exciting ways in which it has cross-fertilised art and business to the mutual benefit of both. During the past decade, Sheeran Lock has created art exhibitions, competitions, events, and education programmes which have touched upon many key issues of our time. Themes have included environment and conservation; cultural identity; the hopes and fears of young people; the physical and emotional impact of serious illness; and the practice and appreciation of art for a balanced life. www.sheeranlock.com

Qua Tendis Ltd is a UK-based joint venture facilitator which helps businesses in developing countries to find business partners in developed countries and vice versa. Rather than focusing on securing venture capital, Qua Tendis specialises in identifying sound business propositions which require specialist, outside skills and knowledge to ensure business sustainability and profitability. It then works to create strategic alliances with companies in those countries which benefit both partners and lead to the creation of sustainable wealth and growth in countries where few such opportunities exist.